A WALK ON THE BEACH

A WALK ON THE BEACH

sermons

by

HARRY B. SCHOLEFIELD
D.D.

MINISTER FIRST UNITARIAN UNIVERSALIST CHURCH
SAN FRANCISCO 1957-1973
MINISTER EMERITUS SINCE 1973

FIRST UNITARIAN UNIVERSALIST CHURCH

SAN FRANCISCO

Copyright © 1999 Harry B. Scholefield, D.D.
Published by
First Unitarian Universalist Church of San Francisco
1187 Franklin Street
San Francisco, CA
94109-6893

Cover photograph by Sally Larsen

ISBN 0-9673663-9-9

First Edition

Contents

Foreword	11
Introduction	13

The Sermons

A Walk on the Beach	15
Why I am a Unitarian	19

Reflections

Rabindranath Tagore's *Gitanjali* I	31
Rabindranath Tagore's *Gitanjali* II	41
Rabindranath Tagore's *Gitanjali* III	51
Rabindranath Tagore's *Gitanjali* IV	61
The Flowering of the Spirit	71
The Need for Non-Violent Dissent in the Streets	81
Peace and Our Blindness	91

Selfhood

Self-Discovery	105
Self-Growth	115
Our Unconscious Selves	125
Self-Actualization in Tough Circumstances	135
The Faith of Sigmund Freud	145

GROWING TOWARDS PERSONHOOD

Deep Decision Making	159
Willing and Choosing	169
Attention is I Can	177
Notes on Inner Space Travel	185
Let the Congregations Speak	195
Witness for Life	205
Unitarians are Eggheads	211
What I Hear Myself Saying	219
Prayers That Stick to My Ribs	229
Think, Thank, Act!	237
Psychoanalysis and the Parish Ministry	241

FOREWORD

I met Harry Scholefield in 1954. He was the minister at the First Unitarian Church of Philadelphia — I was a freshman at the University of Pennsylvania. I moved to San Francisco in early 1959, and there he was again — as minister at the First Unitarian Church of San Francisco. Harry presided over a two or three evening class on Unitarianism which I attended. After class, we would go out for a beer.

My life was such that by the time Sunday came around, I was pretty much worn out by the normal routine of everyday living. But no matter how Sunday began, I always left church feeling a bit taller and more than ready to take on whatever might be ahead.

From Harry's sermons I developed a very deep sense of ethical values. He taught me the importance of truth and the value of choice. I learned to respect a searching, doubting, questioning mind. Harry Scholefield taught me to be a healthy skeptic, but never a cynic. He taught me that religion is not so much a matter of what you say you believe, but how you lead your life.

The two major contributors who helped me develop my moral compass were my father and Harry. As I look back over my life, one of my serious regrets is that I didn't get on with it, go to church and hear Harry more often. I am sure I would have been the better for it. And I am sure there are thousands of others out there who have been equally inspired by Harry's thoughts.

This collection came about in a curious way. While meeting with Margot Campbell Gross, co-minister of the First Unitarian Universalist Church of San Francisco, I asked if there were reprints or any sort of collection of Harry's sermons. She said, "No, there isn't."

"Well then, why don't you call Harry and see what he thinks about getting one together," I proposed. She did. Harry said yes, and here we are.

Working with Harry on this collection has been one of the most fun and fulfilling projects of my life. At our first meeting (Margo, Harry and I), we reviewed Harry's candidates for inclusion in the book. Harry went on to describe how every minister has only one sermon or message: "Mine was hope."

My immediate response was, "Harry, after all these years, I get it." *Hope* was the runner-up for the title of this collection. We had some spirited conversations on what to include and what to take out. At the end of the day, these are Harry's true favorites. We hope you enjoy this *walk on the beach*.

I am personally and deeply indebted to Charles Wehrenberg, Bart Alberti and Sally Larsen for doing all the things that transform a collection of mimeographed pages into the book you have before you. Thanks guys.

Harry, this one is for you.

george a. miller

INTRODUCTION

It is with pride and pleasure we offer these collected sermons by our Minister Emeritus, Harry Scholefield, on the occasion of the Sesquicentennial of the First Unitarian Universalist Society of San Francisco, the church he served from 1957-1973.

I am very grateful to a member of the congregation, George Miller, for his enthusiastic, and tireless, pursuit of the project. Many years ago Harry's sermons inspired George. Publishing this book has been made possible by George's generosity, and his faith in the message of hope that he heard in the sermons.

Reading this book, may we feel renewed by the wisdom and love found in these sermons by Harry Scholefield.

Margot Campbell Gross
co-minister of the First Unitarian Universalist Church of San Francisco

the sermons

A WALK ON A BEACH

........Perhaps
The truth depends on a walk around a lake,

A composing as the body tires, a stop
To see hepatica, a stop to watch
A definition growing certain and

A wait that certainty, a rest
In the swags of pine trees bordering the lake.
Perhaps there are times of inherent excellence,

As when the cock crows on the left and all
Is well, incalculable balances,
At which a kind of Swiss perfection comes

And a familiar music of the machine
Sets up its Schwärmerei, not balances
That we achieve but balances that happen,

As a man and woman meet and love forthwith.
Perhaps there are moments of awakening,
Extreme, fortuitous, personal, in which

We more than awaken, sit on the edge of sleep,
As on an elevation, and behold
The academies like structures in a mist.

One of the memorable experiences I had this past summer was a walk on a beach north of Boston in Gloucester, Mass. It is called Good Harbor Beach and it is a favorite beach of mine. I first made its acquaintance in 1938 when I went to Gloucester as Minister of the First Parish.

The date was July 10th, three months ago. But that doesn't matter because the kind of experience I am talking about is strangely indifferent to calendars. An aspect of the experience is a sense of timelessness. It was early in the morning at sunrise. The beach was strikingly beautiful, peaceful.

As I walked, I was struck with the untouched, pristine expanse of beautiful sand. It was low tide and the outgoing tide had swept everything clean, so the beach was completely unmarked.

New creation—new beginnings, unspoiled openness were strong impressions that came to my mind.

I had the feeling that it was a new day in a fresh world and that I, in my inmost being, was partaking, drinking of the freshness and newness.

The tide was turning, beginning to come in on the beach. It gave me a sense of the tides in my own life, the good tides of love and faith and hope were also turning and coming in with the new day.

I was alone on the beach, and I remember thinking to myself that, if suddenly I had come upon a footprint in the undisturbed expanse of sand, I would have felt a bit like Robinson Crusoe. I would have been Robinson Crusoe without any fear. Robinson Crusoe with wonder.

There was something else that was coming through to me on that beach, but in order to speak to it, I need to back up a bit.

A number of years ago here in San Francisco, a young actress told me she had fallen in love with a young photographer, and that something marvelous had happened to her as a result. "He is," she said, "restoring to me the gift of sight. I know how to listen and I know how to speak. But he is teaching me to see in new ways. When I walk on the beach with him, I see patterns in the sand that I have not seen before. The patterns in the sand were always there with their strange rhythm and beauty, but I wasn't there."

restoring to me the gift of sight

On that morning on Good Harbor Beach, as I looked in the sand, I saw rills, tiny furrows. They seemed exactly like the veins in my forearms. I knew then that the great cosmic stream of life was flowing through the sand as it was flowing through my body.

Not surprisingly, there came into my consciousness some lines of the poet Rabindranath Tagore on which I had been meditating days earlier. "The same stream of life that runs through my veins night and day runs through the world and dances in rhythmic measures. It is the same life that is rocked in the ocean cradle of birth and death, of ebb and flow."

I then became aware that I was not alone on that beach—the young woman, the actress, was walking with me, though I had forgotten her name, and her friend the photographer—I never knew his name—and Rabindranath Tagore, and then others, like Duke Ellington. These words of his came back to me around the compelling freshness of the day. "Every morning you wake up it's a new day, isn't it? Is there any reason why people shouldn't be influenced by a new day?" The Duke was walking with me. And the naturalist, Donald Culross Peattie, and words of his which described me as I walked by the sea: "A handful of supple earth, and long white stones, with sea water running in your veins."

Now as I walked along the beach I was no longer alone, though I did love being alone. I was surrounded by many people, and distinctions between the living and the dead has disappeared. The dead were also the living and I was in touch with them. For a bit of time, I did not differentiate my own being from the being of the sea, the sand, the sea gulls and the sky, the flowing of life in my own veins from the flowing ocean tides. We were all one.

For just a few moments, I experienced unitive consciousness, ecstacy. The word "ecstacy" is derived from two Greek words—one meaning "out of" or "beside," the other meaning "to stand." It means to be beside one's self. It means to be simultaneously in the world and out of the world.

Wallace Stevens has a point. Perhaps the truth depends on a walk on the beach.

*****

NOTE

Perhaps by Wallace Stevens from *The Palm at the End of the Road: Selected Poems*, Vintage Books, 1982, pp. 212-213

WHY I AM A UNITARIAN

[THIS SERMON WAS GIVEN PRIOR TO THE MERGER OF THE UNITARIAN AND UNIVERSALIST CHURCHES.]

On the face of it, there should be few easier tasks than the task of setting forth our religious beliefs and telling how those beliefs came to be central in our thinking and feeling. For most of us, however, the undertaking is difficult. It is difficult to separate essentials from nonessentials. It is difficult to be completely honest. It is never easy when we are dealing with religious feelings and idealism to say where rationalization begins and ends. It is easy to write an intellectual argument defending our point of view on rational grounds, but overlooking completely the existence and the demands of the unconscious.

Our adult religion is always deeply conditioned by early childhood experiences. Many of these experiences are nonetheless potent because they are beyond the recall of memory. I am not here concerned with my own earliest experiences, though I recognize their primary importance. The story which I wish to tell begins with those elements in my background which were dominant from the age of nine to seventeen. During these years, I attended a school strongly oriented in the direction of Evangelical Protestantism with all the elements of strengths and weakness which are a part of this tradition. From them I am sure I derived much which makes me the kind of Unitarian I am or seek to be today.

The emphasis upon formal religion in this school was strong and constant. Each day's school sessions were preceded by devotional exercises at which the Bible was read, hymns were sung, and usually a short homily was delivered. I have always been grateful that, as a child, I was subject to so steady a diet of Bible reading. I find now that the metaphors and texts of the Bible frequently float into my mind as from unknown sources. Actually, a major source must have been those daily devotional services. Every Sunday, except during the summer, we attended the eleven o'clock church school, a church service at two o'clock, and an evening church service. No "cuts" were given as at later college chapel services, and the number of services I missed over an eight-year period was infinitesimally small. In this formal part of our religious experience, stress was placed upon the Bible as the ultimate source of truth and authority. We were expected to accept is as "gospel," although my recollection is that our teachers were primarily interested in "practical religion" and tolerant of our questions and even of our disagreements. The ideal of morality which was presented to us was puritanical in character. The hymns we sang were gospel hymns, sung with warmth and fervor. I think that, even as a child, I was, at times, aware that their warmth and emotionalism contrasted somewhat strangely with the more rugged elements of discipline and practice by which this kind of Protestantism is marked.

Apart from the emphasis upon the Bible as a rule for faith and conduct, I was taught in the school classroom, in the cottage homes, and in various school pursuits, a high degree of respect for the following values. Self-reliance was greatly esteemed and constantly emphasized, although at the same time we were also taught that we were members of a community and that it was our duty always to bear in mind the welfare of the group. There was a paradox here—we were to be always independent in our living and thinking, but never to forget our dependence upon the community of which we were members. The importance of learning and study was the subject of never-ending reiteration, and all of us were expected to enroll in the pre-college course of high school study. There was a place for both work and recreation, although a boy's work was considered the centerpiece of his life. Work was what gave life meaning and purpose. I can still remember singing the hymn, "Work for the night is coming," and cherishing the impression that night was to be thought of as an unwanted and unwelcome intruder, depriving us of the daylight essential to work in the fields. On the other hand, since the school has a spacious campus, including miles of trails through lovely woodlands, I have vivid memories of the beauty of the night, both the early evenings and the very dark winter mornings, when I set about my work milking cows and, for one year when I was fourteen, managing the school dairy.

The keys to self-understanding are to be found in many of the facets of our life which, as children and also as adults, we take for granted. It is against the background so briefly described above that I find keys to some of the doors through which I pass to gain a better understanding of my own motivations. From this background of Evangelical Protestantism and the teachers who embodied it, there was bred in me certain satisfactions and dissatisfactions which were to result in the kind of allegiance I give to Unitarianism. The stress laid upon the importance of academic achievement made books, learning and thinking assume a primary place in my scale of values. To this day, for me there are few beings more endowed with celestial status than the college professor and the thinker—I say this recognizing that the two beings are not always one. At the same time, this emphasis upon the importance of study as a means of getting ahead has made it difficult for me to read books for the sheer joy of reading, or to think for the sake of thinking. I realize that my own reading habits are heavy and that I am very serious in my choice of books. Because of my training, the enjoyment of a pursuit for its own sake is a dangerous business bordering on the immoral! I developed at the school not only habits of self-reliance, but a strong sense of

__Because of my training, the enjoyment of a pursuit for its own sake is a dangerous business__

competitiveness which, while it has advantages in a competitive society, often tends to make one more interested in being superior to his fellows than in understanding and helping them. The stress upon work had obviously favorable results, but in my case it was so dominant an emphasis that, to this day, it is quite impossible for me to enjoy leisure unless I am able to convince myself that the leisure somehow serves to advance my work! Were space not limited, I could mention other aspects of the life at the school which, although they were not directly related to religious training, had much to do with the religious philosophy which I subsequently achieved.

I was always interested in religion. From early years I experienced satisfaction as well as anxiety in public speaking. The satisfaction must have outweighed the anxiety, for I can hardly remember a time when I was not willing to speak, with or without knowledge, on almost any subject! Of all the men I knew in the school, none ranked higher in my esteem or affection that its founder. He was, at the time I attended school, an old man. He had been a minister, but served in the parish ministry only briefly because of his primary interest in the welfare of young people and his desire to work with them. He was a man of great personal magnetism. He had a sense of humor and a love of people which made it impossible for him to keep within narrow denominational lines. He was a gifted speaker as well as an able writer, and a number of his sermon illustrations and stories are quite as clear in my mind now as when he first used them. In the pulpit, he had the happy skill of making his young congregation feel that their maturity was quite on a par with his own. He gave them his respect and affection and they returned the coin in kind.

Always I had been interested in religion, but always I was troubled by the formal aspects of religion as they were set forth in church and church school. Years after I had left the school, I recognized in the words of Edwin Tenney Brewster a statement of one of the major causes of conflict and unhappiness. "Six days a week," writes Brewster, "we live in an ordered world. On the seventh we open the church door on a land of topsy-turvy where axes float, dry sticks change into serpents, cities are let down out of the sky, angels stir the waters of wells, bedeviled swine run violently into the sea. We say prayers asking for rain an hour after we have consulted a government bulletin to see whether we shall need an umbrella before we get home." The teachings of the church school, the emphasis upon the Bible, the atmosphere of the church services were, for me, marked by a curious sense of unreality. On the one hand, I was repelled by the feeling that much of what passed for literal truth in religion was actually myth and fiction—I had not then learned that myth and fiction have a value of their own. On the other hand, I felt that the besetting sin of formal religion, as I experienced it, was not so much that it was wrong, but that it was irrelevant. Church and religion simply did not matter: their concerns were not geared to my problems.

All during this time, however, when I rebelled against religion, I was deeply attracted to it, partly, I suspect, because of the personality and character of the founder of the school whom I have previously mentioned. To the extent that I consciously thought about the dogmas on which Evangelical Protestantism is based, I was mostly in disagreement with them. By the time that I was a senior in high school, I was questioning, in a rather confused and uncertain way, the doctrines of Original Sin, the Atonement, the verbal inspiration of the Bible, the miraculous content of the New Testament as interpreted in terms of the suspension of natural law, the deity of Christ and the Resurrection. I was particularly troubled by the teaching that Jesus was God, and, as such, was to be considered different in kind from all men who had ever lived. It seemed to me that if he was supernaturally endowed by God as the unique Saviour, his life lost much of its significance for ordinary men and women living in a natural world. It was not until years, later when I read Emerson's "Divinity School Address," that my own thought and feeling crystallized and became more clearly defined. Even in high school, it was quite impossible for me to take seriously the idea that a God of love could condemn any-

when I rebelled against religion

one to hellfire. The fact that this was one of the teachings ascribed to Jesus of Nazareth disturbed me more than that it was considered "sound doctrine" in the minds of theologians. It seemed to me then—and it still does seem to me—to be impossible nonsense, no matter on whose authority it is taught.

As I found my disagreement with theological statements and so-called Biblical truths growing more and more marked, the conviction was also growing that, though these statements and truths might be unreal, back of them or beyond them was a Reality which could not be denied. I persisted in believing that, notwithstanding the theology and kind of Biblical interpretation to which I was exposed, nothing was more important and nothing more enduring in human life than an experience of vital religion. Early in life, as a result of a succession of tragedies which struck my family with what must have seemed to me as a child, a relentless and bewildering cruelty, I had become aware of the dangerous nature of the world in which I lived. At the age of ten, I feel sure that the line from Ecclesiastes, "Vanity of vanities, all is vanity," would have struck an echoing response in my mind and heart. I think I was more than a little like the early mariners who, believing that the world was flat, lived in terror lest, sailing too far, they might tumble off the world's edge to destruction below. There was something of this fear in my early life and, though its effect was far from being altogether beneficial, it may have had beneficent results. Since life was so uncertain an undertaking, I felt that I must find some abiding certainties to which I could anchor my existence. No doubt this played a part in my choice of the ministry as a profession.

From the rather limited confines of this school, I went to a fine liberal arts college which, of course, granted to its students a much larger measure of freedom than that to which I had been accustomed. This was for me a momentous change and naturally I used my freedom for purposes of rebellion. I rarely attended services in the college chapel, partly because I was earning my way through college and carrying a heavy burden of work in addition to academic responsibilities, and partly because I was in strong rebellion against religion in its formalized aspects. In my junior year I entered into a friendship with the minister of the college church, a Congregationalist. So skeptical was I, at this time, of the value of the ministry and the Church that I doubt that he would have been acceptable to me as a friend had he not been highly praised by men on the college faculty for whom I had unbounded respect and admiration. His eyesight was failing, and occasionally some of the college students as well as some of the professors read to him. This service was esteemed a privilege, and I volunteered to read. I cannot remember what we read apart from some of the longer poems by John Masefield. In the course of our sessions together, we talked about theology and religion. He quickly sensed the religious content of my skepticism and the meaning of my rebellion. One day, as I paraded my manifold doubts before him, he remarked quietly that I sounded like a Unitarian! He was wise enough not to suggest directly that I go into the ministry. He did suggest, however, that I go to the school which he had attended, the Harvard Divinity School, in order to assure myself that my skepticism was well-founded and that the ministry had no appeal for me. This was exactly the kind of rationalization I needed, and following graduation from college, I entered Harvard Divinity School. While Harvard Divinity School is nonsectarian in character, it has a great deal of Unitarianism in its tradition. I was quickly led into an association with the Unitarian ministers and with Unitarian churches. In 1936 I became a member of the Arlington Street Church in Boston, the church of William Ellery Channing.

The motives with which I joined this historic Unitarian Church were as mixed as our motives usually are. I was a Protestant in the negative sense that I knew what I was against. I knew what I did *not* believe. But I was only beginning to sense the affirmative meanings of the word "Protestant": "To protest on behalf of"..."to testify for"..."to affirm." Over the past twenty years, I have gradually begun to shape some of the "positives" which make my life worth living.

They are my lodestars. I shall try to summarize them here, recognizing as I do so that what follows will be an awkward and inadequate statement of my credo.

I believe that a man's real religion usually lies underneath the formal theology he professes and is not rooted in the creeds which he recites. It is rooted in those qualities of life which are at the center of the network of relationships by which his life is comprised: his relationship to himself, his relationship to others and his relationship to the vast universe of which his life is so infinitesimally small a fragment.

he remarked quietly that I sounded like a Unitarian!

I believe that more "religious" than the act of assent to the creed or theology of any church is the experience of awe and wonder in the face of life's ongoing mysteries. This is not to deny the pragmatic function of creeds and theologies. It is to affirm that they are manmade, and witness more to man's need to see meaning and purpose in life than to any final knowledge of the nature of Deity. They are husks of the grain. "To get a crop," as Sri Ramakrishna puts it, "one must needs sow grain with the husk on, but if one wants to get at the kernel itself, he must remove the husk of the grain." I believe that a true experience of God is revealed in lives marked by love and service rather than the acceptance of close-knit systems or of ancient creeds.

I am convinced that the practice of making "belief in God" the text by which religious persons are separated from the irreligious, is misleading and harmful, for the word of God is a basket into which every conceivable interpretation of life has been poured. Whether men are prepared to say that they believe in God is of small consequence compared to whether or not their lives are marked by altruism and understanding. It is too easy to make belief in God a shibboleth, a test of conformity by which the sheep are separated from the goats, a means of indulging deep and irrational prejudices. The charge of blasphemy, or what we today would call "atheism," has often been used by the narrowly orthodox against the most deeply religious of men. Jesus of Nazareth—and his experience echoes that of earlier prophets and philosophers—was considered blasphemous by his orthodox contemporaries!

I believe that man has nothing to fear and everything to gain from the fullest possible use of reason and mind. Insofar as science and religion are both concerned with the discovery of truth, there is no difference between them. In some ways, science appears to be much more religious than what often passes for religion. Insofar as religion is concerned with the truth, it must welcome and encourage the searching, doubting, questioning mind; for where there is distrust of the mind, there is distrust of both God and man.

I believe in the power of dreams

I believe in the power of dreams. I believe that life is more than logic. Man's ancient dreams of a wiser humanity and a better society represent a major contribution of religion to our well-being. Far from being "illusions," the products of wishful thinking, these dreams are potent realities helping to shape and determine the "facts" of man's existence.

I believe in religion as a way of life rather than a system of belief, and that nothing constitutes a better starting point for the building of a profoundly religious attitude than respect for the dignity and individuality of all men. I believe that the most sensitively religious men and women of our generation are those who, irrespective of whether or not they belong to the churches and synagogues, are working with might and main against the threat of war and all the root causes in society which make for war.

I believe that religion is more than morality. It is music, rite, ritual, symbol and celebration. I believe that the constructive use of symbols and myths is a mark of great wisdom. But "conscience in action" is always the touchstone of prophetic religion, and the gospel which is not a social gospel is but half a religion.

I believe that religion stems from the unconscious as well as the conscious part of man's nature, and that the importance of this fact will be made increasingly clear in the years which lie just ahead.

I believe that science, by enlarging our understanding of the universe and by bringing us new insights into the nature of human nature, renders priceless services to the cause of religion. It helps us to understand religion's irrational elements. It will help us to understand the function of imagination as well as the function of reason, and, through this understanding, to free religion of its elements of fear and superstition.

I believe that all religions are links in one chain, and I am at least beginning to understand what F. Max Muller meant by his statement: "There never was a false god, nor was there ever really a false religion unless you call a child a false man."

I believe that no law of life is more self-evident than the law of change and growth, and that this law applies to theology as well as to all human disciplines. This truth is perhaps more appreciated by the leaders of Hinduism than by Christian leadership. At any rate, it is eloquently illustrated in the lines written by Sarvepalli Radakrishnan: "We must preserve the precious substance of religious reality by translating it out of the moods and thoughts of other times into terms and needs of our own day and generation.... Time changes all things and the Spirit in us must guide us into all truth."

I was first led to Unitarianism by my disagreement with the orthodox theology of my childhood. I have learned now to look upon that theology with more understanding than when I first rebelled against it. I have also learned that one cannot build a strong religion out of disagreements alone. I have learned these lessons and many others in the Unitarian Fellowship. I am a Unitarian today because for me it has proven to be a fellowship exceedingly rich in the values which unite. I have found it an open door through which I may pass to a quickened appreciation of the good in all religions and all generations. I have come to prize this fellowship the more because it welcomes and encourages diversity of theological beliefs and liturgical practices. It helps me to relate my life to those inclusive, ongoing, liberal traditions of the race which are as old as the history of man. It inspires me to look for the light yet to break. It gives me new faith in myself. It speaks to my deepest hopes and fears, saying: "The world is round. Sail as far as you will in search of truth. You will encounter storms; you may be wrecked. But in the long run, the universe is on the side of those who trust their own minds, value supremely their own experiences, and dare to sail under their own true colors."

REFLECTIONS ON RABINDRANATH TAGORE'S "GITANJALI"

I

Many of us have had the experience of driving toward the Rockies on a clear day and feeling they were so near we could reach out and touch them with our hands. We discovered, however, as we drove along that they were much further away than we had thought. It was a considerable time before we could actually touch them with our hands. I want to speak on Rabindranath Tagore's little sheaf of songs called, *Gitanjali*. I will be lucky, however, if I even reach the Songs this morning. I found in thinking about them that there was much I wanted to say before I could actually touch them.

There is a disease which is extremely widespread in our times. It can be given many different names. It might be called "consumeritis," "super-activism," "debilitating busy-ness," or simply "inner emptiness." It can be compared to a psychological state in which we eat lots of nourishing food, but are unable to get nourishment from what we take in. It appears that the chemical processes of the body are somehow out of order, so that the nutriment we take in is destroyed or rejected before it does any good. Our curious dilemma is that the more we eat the less we are nourished.

All of us fall into this state. When I am in it I am prone to compare myself—that is, my state of being or non-being—with a line from the *Rhyme of the Ancient Mariner*—WATER, WATER EVERYWHERE BUT NOT A DROP TO DRINK. Or I am prone to identify myself with the fabled King Midas who was given the power to turn to gold everything he touched. This was his wish. Everything he touched did turn to gold. He became imprisoned in gold and was eventually destroyed by his own greed. His greed, it turned out, was his character, and his character was his fate.

Sometimes in moments of candor we say to one another or to ourselves, "I am impoverished inside myself." "I live, but I do not live." "I have lost my capacity to experience joy in myself and in the world."

Now when we fall into this state we have many ways of rationalizing our situation. We say it is that we are the victim of harsh outer circumstances. But it will not do—at least not in my book—to say that the world is "in such a mess, in such a mess, in such a mess," that only a fool or only an ultra-selfish person could find any joy in it. This misses an essential point about the nature of existence, namely, that in the most sensitive persons, the strongest persons, joy is not the same thing as satisfaction with external circumstances.

joy is not the same thing as satisfaction with external circumstances.

Part of our dilemma, I believe, is that we have developed the bad habit of identifying our fate, our lives, too much with externalities—saying, "I could be happy if such and such a condition characterized my outside world—if I were married to the right woman or to the right man, if my children behaved so and so, if my business were in good condition, if I were able to attain such and such a place of distinction in my profession." We are always overlooking the fact that if we want to use the word, "circumstances," in its full sense, then we must recognize that our psyche is a part of our circumstances, our posture to the world, our hopes and expectations, our fears, our hatreds, our loves, our likes and dislikes, our warmth and our coldness are all part of our circumstances.

To interpret or understand circumstances simply in terms of externalities is to miss the most important part of reality. The inward attitude revealed essentially in expectations, consciously cultivated but rooted in the unconscious, does not merely alter our circumstances—it is indeed an integral part of them.

It has been said that every man's life is based on a particular fairy tale, and that if we know enough about that man, we can recognize the fairy tale which is the key to his character. I would say that there is a prayer in every man's life, and that if we know the content and nature of that prayer we know the man at his deepest levels. Our real prayer is our hopes and fears, our expectations, our loves and hates.

there is a prayer in every man's life

Each of us has certain basic expectations of every day that we live. Perhaps it may shock some people to hear this said, but I believe it can be argued that in this sense everyone of us starts every single day of our lives with a prayer. The admonition of St. Paul that we should pray without ceasing, taken in this sense, is not as far fetched as it seems. Indeed, it is literally true. We can dispense with the language of formal theology in this matter and cultivate a psychological understanding. Our prayer is rooted in our patterns of willing and of wishing. There is a strong relationship between wishing and praying. I am not sure that it has ever been fully explored.

Our prayers may be as much revealed in our physical postures as in any other way. So with this question of the manner in which we greet the new day. Sometimes we greet it with our arm up defensively, or with our hands up like a policeman's hands directed toward stopping traffic. Sometimes we greet the new day with our hands open in a welcoming gesture. It is important that we become conscious of the reality of these gestures. It will help us to comprehend more fully the meaning of what we call "our circumstances," if we are conscious, not to begin with, with the content of our longings, but if we are conscious simply of their existence and of their profound relevance to the totality of our experience.

Sometimes these longings get articulated in words. It appears to be an ineradicable desire to find moving, meaningful words in which these longings can be expressed. Sometimes they are our own words, clumsy perhaps, at least personal longing and our own. A number of years ago I tried to articulate my basic longing, my basic wish and it took the form of these words:

Help me to affirm the gift of life in myself and others and to know myself affirmed.

When I couch the words in this "help me" frame of reference I am recognizing my dependence upon others and upon the universe of which I am a part. Sometimes I say simply:

I affirm the gift of life in myself and others and I know myself affirmed.

This is a conscious effort on my part to articulate a very basic longing—how important it is that we affirm the gift of life and how enormously important it is that we know ourselves affirmed by others. There are times when we lose our capacity to affirm ourselves. Then it appears that knowledge that we are affirmed by others is one of the few kinds of knowledge that can restore self-affirmation.

At times, we try to put these longings in our own words. At other times we take hold of words that are very, very ancient and let them speak for us.

The other day I ran across this passage in the writing of José Ortega y Gasset, the brilliant Spanish philosopher. He has been writing of the importance of the quest for understanding. He speaks of the religious nature of understanding:

"There is a true religious attitude at the center of the urge to understand, and, as far as I am concerned, I must confess that when I get up in the morning, I recite a very brief prayer, thousands of years old, a verse from the *Rig Veda* which contains these few winged words: 'Lord, awaken us in a happy mood and give us knowledge.' Thus prepared I go through the bright or gloomy hours that come with the day."

This act of Ortega's I would call looking toward the inward state. The attitude in itself reminds us that we have a capacity for wisdom, which needs to be cultivated and which is not in the subject-object relationship to "our circumstances" but is an essential part of them. The ancients were right when they stressed the importance of what they called "spiritual resources."

> *spiritual resources can not be understood simply as an object of cultivation*

These spiritual resources cannot be understood simply as an object of cultivation. Sometimes they are more like what it today called "a happening."

A woman who lost her child through a tragic accident told me that at first the tragedy shocked her into a kind of mute grief. But several days after the tragedy she experienced a sense of inner peace so profound that it changed her grief into a deeper acceptance of life. When I talked with her several years after the death of her child, she still felt the power of this experience in which grief was transmuted into inner peace, though she could not explain it or say how it had come to pass. All she knew was that it had become a vital part of her consciousness.

Many of us, thank God, have had experiences of this sort. As I try to understand them, and certainly they are not completely comprehensible, certain elements in them come clear. Let me mention two of these elements.

First is what I started to underscore a few moments ago. Peace of mind, the experience of joy even in the aftermath of tragedy—this is only partly contingent upon external circumstances. The more we understand these things, the more it appears that a most important part of "our circumstances" is what traditionally has been called, "spiritual resources," "the inner life." I believe the psychologists call it "intrapsychic organization." The moralist calls it strength of character.

Secondly, it appears to me that—and here an act of faith is involved, a forward movement that isn't simply a matter of logic—whether we feel our ultimate destiny is death or new and unpredictable forms of life, we are, in either case, involved in processes which have a creative dimension. At times the creative dimension is unlocked or is released by tragedies which one might think would destroy creativity.

Here are some words from Norman Brown's book, *Love's Body*, which bear on the point:

"Freedom is fire, overcoming this world by reducing it to a fluctuating chaos, as in schizophrenia; the chaos which is the eternal ground of creation. There is no universe, no one way."

....

We are always in error,
Lost in the wood
Standing in chaos
The original mess
Creating a brand new world.

....

"Thank God the world cannot be made safe for democracy or anything else."

Now it is about at this point that the sheaf of Songs of Tagore's *Gitanjali* comes into play. The word *"Gitanjali"* means handful of songs or garland of songs. These songs were written by one of the great men of the Twentieth Century who had a particular posture toward life, a particularly self-fulfilling life stance. He demonstrated in his living a full realization of how the inner state of a man is a part of his circumstances.

A song, painting or any work of art can stand on its own legs as a work of art. But to me the meaning of a song, poem or painting deepens as I come to appreciate the context out of which the work of art arose. It may be a weakness on my part but I am historically oriented, biographically oriented in these matters. When I first began to utilize the beautiful songs of Tagore as a means of deepening my own life-intentions; as a means of lifting up my devotion; as a means of letting more music break through into my devotional life; as a mode of articulating various feelings about my existence; I was only secondarily concerned with their originator. Then as the songs became more a part of me, I found I wanted to know more about the man who wrote them, and more about the soil from which they grew. So I found myself reading and pondering over Krishna Kripalani's biography of Rabindranath Tagore. So at an early date I will want to share with you some of my feelings about that biography.

> *the meaning of a song, poem or painting deepens as I come to appreciate the context out of which the work of art arose*

But now, going back to the illustration I used at the beginning, we have driven through the foothills and are approaching some mountains. Now I will read to you three of the songs of Tagore taken from *Gitanjali*. They will, of course, speak for themselves. These songs do not have titles, but as one comes to meditate on them and absorb them they have salient characteristics that stand out and they appeal to certain specific conditions of the human spirit. The first song I will read reflects the spirit of a man at a point where hope is latent but not yet realized. The second song is very remarkable in my judgment because in so few words it touches very graphically several states of mind and spirit with which we are all familiar. The third song is perhaps better understood if we bear in mind the Hindu teaching of reincarnation, but not really, for the state of emptiness and fullness which it describes embodies universal experience.

The song that I came to sing remains unsung to this day. I have spent my days in stringing and unstringing my instrument.

The time has not come true, the words have not been rightly set; only there is the agony of wishing in my heart.

The blossom has not opened; only the wind is sighing by.

I have not seen his face, nor have I listened to his voice; only I have heard his gentle footsteps from the road before my house.

The livelong day has passed in spreading his seat on the floor; but the lamp has not been lit and I cannot ask him into my house.

I live in the hope of meeting with him; but this meeting is not yet.

***

When the heart is hard and parched up, come upon me with a shower of mercy.

When grace is lost from life, come with a burst of song.

When tumultuous work raises its din on all sides shutting me out from beyond, come to me, my lord of silence, with thy peace and rest.

When my beggarly heart sits crouched, shut up in a corner, break open the door, my king, and come with thy light and thy thunder.

***

Thou hast made me endless, such is thy pleasure. This frail vessel thou emptiest again and again, and fillest it ever with fresh life.

This little flute of a reed thou hast carried over hills and dales, and hast breathed through it melodies eternally new.

At the immortal touch of thy hands my little heart loses its limits in joy and gives birth to utterance ineffable.

Thy infinite gifts come to me only on these very small hands of mine. Ages pass, and still thou pourest, and still there is room to fill.

*****

NOTES

1. *GITANJALI, Song Offerings* by Rabindranath Tagore, with an introduction by William Butler Yeats, International Pocket Library, Boston, Reprinted by special arrangement with the MacMillan Company.

2. Tagore, *A Biography of Rabindranath Tagore* by Krishna Kripalani, Grove Press, Inc., 1962.

3. *Meditations on Quixote* by Ortega y Gasset, W.W. Norton & Company, Inc., New York, 1961.

4. *Love's Body* by Norman O. Brown, Vintage Books, Random House, New York, 1966.

REFLECTIONS ON RABINRANATH TAGORE'S "GITANJALI"
II

I am speaking again this morning on the little sheaf of songs by the great Indian mystic and poet, Rabindranath Tagore. In my first talk on *Gitanjali* I said that central to every person's life is a deep longing which can be described in many ways. It can be called expectation, or intention, or *the deep wish*. It can be called prayer, if prayer is thought of as the conscious and unconscious thrust of mind and spirit. It has been said that the "capacity for intentional self-transcendence"[1] is a primary mark of man. The longing for self-transcendence is expressed in many ways. Certainly it is not expressed in words alone. It is expressed in every art form and is expressed in a thousand different ways in our day to day existence. Tagore himself said, "Nothing is more beautiful or greater than to perform the ordinary duties of one's daily life simply and naturally."[2] It is expressed when we live simply and naturally. But it is expressed in words, and Tagore's Songs are remarkable expressions of it. I won't speak of his plays, short stories or longer poems. I am not very familiar with them.

I like to root a man's creative works in his life. Actually for me Tagore's Songs stand on their own feet. I have reflected on them so often that I can repeat many of them from memory, and their phrases come to me as easily and naturally as do the phrases of Psalms and

Scriptural verses which I learned in childhood. They are familiar words, beloved words. And I have immersed them as deeply as I can in my own thoughts and experiences. They do not stand on their own. But to catch further meanings of them, I have looked to the story of Tagore's life, seeking to see what kind of soil they grew from—whence the inspiration, whence these singular pieces of feeling and enlightenment.

This morning I would like to speak about Tagore's life. I suppose that in a rough sort of way you can separate a man's private life from his public life. This morning I will be reflecting on his "private" life. Perhaps next Sunday, or on some subsequent Sunday, I will reflect on the ways in which he related to the social problems of the tempestuous times in which he lived. We must not forget that he lived at a time when his nation was struggling for its independence and in his own way entered into that struggle. It is, of course, impossible to separate the two life-spheres, private and social, in any complete sense. We know, for example, at that times Tagore's Songs become songs of social protest. On Christmas Day of 1939 he expressed his dismay and bitterness over World War II in a poem:[3]

Those who struck Him once
in the name of their rulers
are born again in the present age.
They gather in their prayer halls
in a pious garb,

> *They call their soldiers*
> *'Kill, Kill' they shout;*
> *in their roaring mingles*
> *while the Son of Man in*
> *His agony prays, 'O God,*
> *fling, fling far away*
> *this cup with the*
> *bitterest of poisons.*

Tagore was born in 1861 and died in 1941 at the age of eighty. This is a long life, particularly in India where the life-expectancy is short. His life paralleled and criss-crossed the life of Gandhi, who lived from 1869 to 1948. Gandhi called him the Great Sentinel. He thought of him as one who was the keeper of the inward life and of the very highest standards of his people. Tagore was a member of India's privilege class. His father was wealthy. His grandfather was fabulously wealthy. His father was a remarkable man and in his youth he underwent a religious experience which was to have an immense impact on his life, and its influence was doubtless to be felt in the life of his famous son.

> *one who was the keeper of the inward life and of the very highest standards of his people*

If strict birth control or even loose birth control, had been practiced by his parents, I presume Tagore would never have been born. He was the fourteenth child borne by his mother.

His family life was lived amidst astonishing circumstances, that is, from a western point of view. It was in effect a great clan, where the family—the sons-in-law and the daughters-in-law, came together sharing one another's joys and sorrows. The description given of it reminds me of a wealthy Chinese family's mode of living as described by Pearl Buck in *The Good Earth*.

It is worth noting that Tagore was a drop-out from school at the age of fourteen. The way he felt about his schooling was very similar to the feelings expressed by some of our own children. He considered it a hospital and a jail. So final was his resolve not to go to school that those responsible for him felt bound to acquiesce in his decision. But what lamentations! His eldest sister who had nursed him as a baby lamented, "We had all hoped Rabi would grow up to be a man, but he has disappointed us the worst."

Sixty-five years after he dropped out of school, he was to write an amusing letter to his grandchild, Nandita. She was taking university entrance exams. He expressed the hope that she would fail in her exams, "for how," he asked, "would he show his face to the world if his grandchild succeeded where he had not."

The reason he dropped out of school was not that he did not believe in education, but because he believed, even at the age of fourteen, that the kind of education he was getting did not promote his growth but hampered it. Later on he was to found a school which would be extremely progressive for its period, and would have a great deal of influence on education. As a matter of fact, Kripalani says that for much of his life he was a school master. It is true that had he not been so gifted in so many other ways he would be more widely known as an outstanding educator.

After he dropped out of school his education became the responsibility of a gifted older brother. His brother was open and relaxed in his pedagogy. We can illustrate this by one example. At the age of fourteen Tagore's poetic gifts were already budding. At this time he wrote his first long narrative poem called, "Wild Flower." It ran to eight cantos, 1600 lines, and was published. At this time, too, Tagore conceived the idea, befitting to a romantic young poet, that he would like to write not in ordinary ink, but with the perfumed extract of flowers. He designed a mechanism by which a pestle would revolve in a big cup-shaped wooden sieve, pressing out the juices of the flowers. He told his brother of his desires and design, and the brother assigned a mechanic to help the boy carry out his wishes. The machine was made to Tagore's specifications but unfortunately it produced only a sodden mass of flowers and mud: so Tagore went back to writing with regular ink. But he was very grateful to his brother for letting him learn through his own failures.

> "My brother Jyotirinda unreservedly let me go my own way to self-knowledge, and only since then could my nature prepare to put forth its thorns, it may be, but likewise, its flowers. This experience of mine has led me to dread, not so much evil itself, as tyrannical attempts to create goodness. Of punitive police, political or moral, I have a wholesome horror.

The state of slavery which is thus brought on is the worst form of cancer to which humanity is subject."[4]

Very early Tagore became aware that deep learning, true learning and true growth comes through direct openness to one's own feelings, openness to other persons, and openness to the world of nature in which we live. Growth of an integral character is not imposed from the outside, it is an unfolding of feelings and perceptions from within. In Tagore growth-awareness of the inner life and awareness of the world "outside" go hand in hand. We open ourselves to

direct openness to one's own feelings, openness to other persons, and openness to the world of nature

what is in us and about us, and in the resultant dialogue, as it were, between the inner spirit and the spirit of the world a mature consciousness grows.

We could illustrate this dialogue in feelings and perceptions coming from it in many ways. I would like to touch on it briefly by referring to Tagore's feelings about space. We have become increasingly conscious of space because of recent technological events, the landing of men on the Moon, the projection of travels to Mars, etc. We know now our Earth is a tiny, beautiful globe floating in limitless space. There is not other generation of man which could have known this fact in the way we know it.

It is said that the Seventeenth Century French religious philosopher and mathematician, Blaise Pascal, was frightened by "the silence of infinite space." It is worth noting that Tagore has an awareness of the "silence of infinite space" which is characterized by joyous acceptance rather than by fear. There are a number of his songs in which this joy in the face of the mystery of space breaks through. One is the 67th Song of *Gitanjali*[5] In this song we also have an example of how Tagore bestows upon God a wide variety of names. Here God becomes the sky and also the nest.

Thou are the sky and thou art the nest as well.

Oh thou beautiful, there in the nest it is thy love that encloses the soul with colors and sounds and odors.

There comes the morning with the golden basket in her right hand bearing the wreath of beauty, silently to crown the earth.

And there comes the evening over the lonely meadows deserted by herds, through trackless paths, carrying cool draughts of peace in her golden pitcher from the western ocean of rest.

But there, where spreads the infinite sky for the soul to take her flight in, reigns the stainless white radiance. There is no day or night, nor form nor color and never, never, never a word.

The 12th song in *Gitanjali* is marvelously rich in imagery suited to a space age. Indeed, I think a journeying astronaut might be hard put to it to discover any song more relevant in the Hebrew-Christian Bible.

The time that my journey takes is long and the way of it long.

I came out on the chariot of the first gleam of light, and pursued my voyage through the wildernesses of worlds leaving my track on many a star and planet.

It is the most distant course that comes nearest to thyself, and that training is the most intricate which leads to the utter simplicity of a tune.

The traveller has to knock at every alien door to come to his own, and one has to wander through all the outer worlds to reach the innermost shrine at the end.

My eyes strayed far and wide before I shut them and said, "Here are thou!"

> *The question and the cry "Oh, where?" melt into tears of a thousand streams and deluge the world with the flood of the assurance "I am!"* [6]

Tagore was a thinker, an intellectual, but an intellectual who was deeply critical of what his biographer, Krishna Kripalani, calls "the academic itch to understand everything."[7] I suppose that the relationship between explaining experience and appreciating it, between full and partial relationships remains a mystery. I always liked those words of Eric Gill, "Good Lord! the thing was a mystery and we measured it."[8] Tagore is skeptical about man's ability to measure everything. In one of his letters he describes an experience which in one way or another will strike home to many of us. It is very late at night. He has been studying an English book on esthetics and beauty. He is working his way through its fine abstractions, definitions and precise explanations. He is getting wearier by the minute; gradually he has the feeling of being tricked, deceived and cheated as he gets lost in the detailed logic of the writer. Finally, he throws the book on the table, blows out the lamp with the intention of retiring immediately. With the lamp out, the room is suddenly flooded with beautiful moon light. He is stunned at the realization that the man-made lamp and the man-made book shut out beauty which was filling the world and said:

> "What had I been looking for in the empty wordiness of the book? There was the very thing itself, filling the skies, silently waiting for me outside all these hours!"[9]

explaining experience and appreciating it, between relationships remains a mystery

Obviously there is a difficult paradox here. We see and we celebrate what we see. We hear and we celebrate what we hear. We seek to understand what we see and what we hear. I do not think that we can put the desire to understand and the appreciate in absolutely opposite camps. They are both part of the same human experience, both in a way the fruit of inward life, but there is a distinction. To celebrate is not the same thing as to explain, and in an age which overemphasizes the "explaining" we do well to call to mind the life and wisdom of one who knew how to celebrate. To sing the beauty of the night sky may not be to explain it, but the singing develops our capacity to celebrate that beauty and the celebration is as essential a part of humanness as explaining. To address the beauty in song is to be addressed by it. There is a dialogue here. And we are greatly enriched whenever we have among us those who know and sing the dialogue.

Tagore, of course, reflected deeply upon this mystery. So in his *My Reminiscences*[10] he is writing on the exaggerated need to understand everything cerebrally. He asks himself about the meaning of poetry and the relationship of poetry to "explanation." Then these words:

> "But does one write poetry to explain any matter? What is felt within the heart tries to find outside shape as a poem. So when, after listening to a poem, anyone says he is not understood, I feel non-plussed. If someone smells a flower and says he does not understand, the reply to him is; there is nothing to understand, it is only a scent.... That words have meaning is just the difficulty. That is why the poet has to turn and twist them in meter and verse, so that the meaning may be held somewhat in check, and the feeling allowed a chance to express itself. This utterance of feeling is not the statement of a fundamental truth, or a scientific fact, or a useful moral precept.... If while crossing a ferry you can catch a fish, you are a lucky man, but that does not make the ferry-boat a fishing boat, nor should you abuse the ferryman if he does not make fishing his business."

does one write poetry to explain any matter?

But there is a song which, at least to me, puts the matter more directly and beautifully. The song is about a flower, the scent of the flower. I didn't select it for that reason. As a matter of fact I am not sure that I selected the song. I have the odd feeling that perhaps the song selected me. It is song number 20 in *Gitanjali*.[11]

On the day when the lotus bloomed, alas, my mind was straying, and I knew it not. My basket was empty and the flower remained unheeded.

Only now and again a sadness fell upon me, and I started up from my dream and felt a sweet trace of a strange fragrance in the south wind.

That vague sweetness made my heart ache with longing and it seemed to me that it was the eager breath of the summer seeking for its completion.

I knew not then that it was so near, that it was mine, and that this perfect sweetness had blossomed in the depth of my own heart.

*****

NOTES

1. Smith, Huston, *Condemned to Meaning*, Harper & Row, 1965.

2. Kripalani, Krishna, *Tagore, A Biography*, Grove Press, Inc., 1962, p. 145.

3. Tagore, *A Biography*, p. 387.

4. Tagore, *A Biography*, p. 65 (quoted from Tagore's *My Reminiscences*).

5. Tagore's *Gitanjali*, Song 67, p. 44.

6. *Gitanjali*, Song 12, p. 17.

7. Tagore, *A Biography*, p. 105.

8. Kerr, Walter, *The Decline of Pleasure*, Simon and Schuster, 1962, p. 202.

9. Tagore, *A Biography*, p. 138. (With regard to Tagore's concern with space, Kripalani quotes Tagore: "Goethe on his death-bed

wanted 'more light.' If I have any desire left at all at such a time, it will be for 'more space' as well.").

10. Tagore, *A Biography*, p. 105.

11. *Gitanjali*, Song 20, page 21.

REFLECTIONS ON RABINDRANATH TAGORE'S "GITANJALI" III

I wish to speak this morning on Rabindranath Tagore's social conscience. He lived through the tumultuous events leading to India's independence. He did not lead a sheltered life. At the time of his death in August, 1941, Gandhi said of him: "There was hardly any activity on which he has not left the impress of his powerful personality."[1] This is especially significant because the Mahatma judged the poet from a unique vantage point. They had their strong differences during their lifetimes. At a later date I would like to speak on their remarkable relationship. The recent publication of Erik Erikson's study of Gandhi, Gandhi's Truth, *On The Origins of Militant Nonviolence*, will constitute unusual source material.[2]

Tagore's social concern stems from the center of his own life. We can look to his Songs for a statement of his humanitarian aspirations. I think specially of the familiar words of Song 36.[3]

> *This is my prayer to thee, my lord—strike, strike at the root of penury in my heart.*
> *Give me the strength lightly to bear my joys and sorrows.*
> *Give me the strength to make my love fruitful in service.*

Give me the strength never to disown the poor or bend my knees before insolent might.

Give me the strength to raise my mind high above daily trifles.

And give me the strength to surrender my strength to thy will with love.

This song is in the form of a prayer. This may put some of us off. But we should remember that this deep yearning to be a person who serves others with deep love is the mark of every person who aspires to be fully human. We need to be clear in our understanding that this is not the crass form of petitionary prayer. It is as different from that as Emerson's teachings about the Oversoul are from Billy Graham's fundamentalist Protestantism.

I hear the poet recognizing his dependency on forces larger than his own life. I hear him confirming his deep desire to establish a relationship to his universe in which his strength is willingly and lovingly given to a Spirit of Wisdom which encompasses and transcends his own particular life.

The message I received here says many things. Here are several of them.

Tagore was his own man in matters of social concern. He was responsible to himself and for himself. He was not a weather vane reflecting the current popular opinion. He was not a fanatic. He subscribed to no "ism." At times he was popular and at times he was unpopular. This was true of his relationship to his own countrymen and it was also true of his relationship to the Japanese, the Americans, the British, etc. But he was human, and he cared whether he was popular or unpopular. He was not thick-skinned. What was it that Mayor Alioto said recently? It was something to the effect that if one was going to be in politics one must be thick-skinned. Tagore was not thick-skinned. Insofar as a politician is one who seeks the power of public office, he was not a politician. On occasion he was filled with a sense of loneliness and sorrow at criticisms that were heaped on his head—criticisms which might come from a wide variety of sources. On one such occasion he wrote the Song:

"They call you mad.
Wait for tomorrow and keep silent.
They throw dust upon your head
Wait for tomorrow,
They will bring their wreath." [4]

There is a saying in American politics—I believe that Harry Truman was its author—"If you can't stand the heat, stay out of the kitchen." There were times when Tagore found it very hard to stand the heat of what we would call confrontation politics. But he did go into the kitchen and he did involve himself *in his own way* in the major political and moral struggles of the day: the struggle for Indian independence, the struggle for peace, the struggle to make men more conscious of their common identity, the struggle against nationalism and racism. Bertrand Russell wrote of him: "He has contributed as much as any man living to the most important work of our time, namely, the promotion of understanding between different races." [5]

But I think the key phrase to describe him at this point is *in his own way*. So when we examine the remarkable friendship and working alliance between Tagore and Gandhi we see it as a tremendous example of how two men can work for the same cause, with profound mutual respect, deep affection, but bringing to the cause different styles and different gifts.

How can we sum up the difference between the two men? It is not easy to say. The poet was not so much a man of action. He did not involve himself so much in specific strategies. In a way he was more "above the battle" than the Mahatma. But in a way he gave those who were in the battle a profound sense of their deeper identity, contributing to the inner resources which helped to sustain them.

At the time of the civil war, Ralph Waldo Emerson published a collection of essays which were beautiful—moving statements of great truths. There were those who criticized him for being too much concerned with eternal truths when men were dying in the fight against slavery, but there were those—actually engaged in the fight—who said that Emerson's thoughts and words gave them hope and the strength to carry on. So it was with the poet, Tagore. He sang of the long range hopes for humanity. He sang of beauty, of love, of awareness of the Divine in the midst of the human. Somehow, his Songs—and of course his character and life—gave strength to those who were more immediately engaged in struggles and tactical aspects of the struggle for freedom.

I think there are no absolute distinctions setting Gandhi's methodologies apart from Tagore's ways, but there are relative distinctions which are also important.

As Tagore participated *in his own way* in the struggle for freedom, he was hurt and he was tormented. He suffered as he sought to understand and ameliorate the tragedies which afflict us. His Songs contain at times a burning indignation against the evils of the day. I call your attention to three songs of this sort.

On Christmas day, 1941, as the Second World War steadily engulfed more and more of mankind, he wrote this song which is a cry against the Western World's perversion of the teachings of Jesus of Nazareth.

Those who struck Him once
in the name of their rulers
are born again in the present age.
They gather in their prayer-halls in a pious garb.
They call their soldiers,
"Kill, Kill," they shout;

*in their roaring mingles
the music of their hymns,
while the Son of Man
in his agony prays,
"O God, fling, fling far away
This cup filled with the bitterest of poisons."*[6]

At about the same time, disillusioned over the militarism of Japan and her cry, "Asia for Asians," he wrote another song. You will note that in the song just referred to he condemns the "Christian" world for its perversion of the teachings of Jesus. Now he condemns the Japanese leaders for their similar betrayal of the teachings of Buddha:

*The war drums are sounded.
Men force their features into frightfulness
and gnash their teeth;
and before they rush out to gather
raw human flesh for death's larder,
they march to the temple of Buddha,
the Compassionate,
to claim his blessings,
while loud beats the drum rat-a-tat
and earth trembles.*[7]

The third song comes out of his disillusionment with the British imperialists, their blindness and brutality in their treatment of India, their failure to perceive the promise of India, and their practice of exploitation. This song is called *Prashan, the Question*. It is not a question to man, however, but a question to God:

You have sent your messengers from time to time who have preached forgiveness and love of all mankind.

They were noble souls and worthy of our reverence, and yet today their message seems a mockery and I want to ask you, 'Are you yourself, O Lord, able to forgive and to love these creatures of yours who have poisoned your air and darkened your light?"[8]

This third poem points to the inner agony and torment which Tagore endured as the other side of his humanitarian concern. Sometimes today faced with the same problems, subject to similar disillusionment and torment we act as though it should be our right to be serene in our concerns for social justice, but Tagore's life says to me there is not way on this road for perfect serenity. One has to experience uncertainty and fear, one has to struggle against disillusionment if one is to live earnestly and seriously in the world.

As a sensitive human being, as well as an artist, creator, singer of songs, he was caught in this very human dilemma. There was a part of him that would like to have pulled back to ways of peace and solitude. There was a part of him that called for involvement in the world wherever there was suffering and injustice. So he traveled, and so he spoke in many parts of the world. He traveled in the USSR by which he was greatly impressed, though he could not subscribe to the Marxist ideology. He saw hope for the poor of India in the struggle against poverty and injustice being waged by the Russian peoples. He traveled in England, in China, in Japan and in many other countries. Everywhere he went he sought to speak universal truths as he understood them and he sought to learn. He was highly concerned with education. So in India he founded a progressive school and a university which is now a state university. Nehru was for a time its president. He wrote songs, plays and stories which very often centered on his country's problems and the world's problems. He did not stand apart. As Gandhi said: "There was hardly any public activity on which he has not left the impress of his powerful personality."[9]

Because *in his own way* and with his own precious gifts, as he entered into struggles of his time, he paid a price in suffering, loneliness, in unrest, in exhaustion and conflict. Always he had faith that when he was true to himself he would be vindicated by time.

They call you mad
Wait for tomorrow and keep silent.
They throw dust upon your head.
Wait for tomorrow,
They will bring their wreath.[10]

Perhaps the truth for us to ponder, though, is that in these struggles—in the barren and empty periods of his life—as in the high moments—in times of success and in times of failure—though he made mistakes and at times exhausted himself—he never lost sense of his own wholeness. He never cut himself off completely from the knowledge that the world, for all its tragedies, renews as well as destroys us. It fills as well as empties. He sang his songs of celebration of life in sorrow and in failure as in joy and triumph. He never gave up his faith in the good potentials of the future.

In the last year of his life when he became terminally ill, he lay in his bed wondering if he had been able to repay the world for the great gift of life.[11] He thought of life as a gift and this says a good deal about his attitude toward life. But even then, when he thought of his own limitations and the shortcomings of his life, he moved beyond them to a vision of the "poet of the unknown multitudes." Thus writing of this poet to come, he spoke these words:

May he give what I lack.
May he save himself from luxury
of mimic sympathy for the laboring people,
which professes what is not its own
trying to achieve that
whose price is dearly paid.
Come poet of the unknown multitudes...
Resuscitate the dormant springs
here they lie hidden
Deep in the heart of our humanity.[12]

Nothing could permanently destroy his faith in the beauty and the promise of the present, in "the dormant springs where they lie hidden deep in the heart of our humanity." Nothing could completely obscure his gratitude for life as a gift. And nothing could put out for long his wondrous capacity for song.

The springs of his inner life being kept open, he was also open to the sources of strength, sources of renewal in the world around him. Out of this kind of self-awareness and world-awareness there came a vision of the future which was always humane at the same time it was revolutionary. Thus there is a straight line which runs between the prayer,

Give me the strength lightly to bear my joys and my sorrows.

Give me the strength to make my love fruitful in service.

Give me the strength never to disown the poor or bend my knees before insolent might.

Give me the strength to raise my mind high above daily trifles.

And such a song of wonder, joy and thanksgiving as Song 63,

Thou has made me known to friends whom I knew not.

Thou has given me seats in homes not my own. Thou has brought the distant near and made a brother of the stranger.

I am uneasy at heart when I have to leave my accustomed shelter; I forget that there abides the old in the new, and that there also thou abidest.

Through birth and death, in this world or in others, whenever thou leadest me it is thou, the same, the one companion of my endless life who ever linkest my heart with bonds of joy to the unfamiliar.

When one knows thee, then alien there is none, then no door is shut. Oh, grant me my prayer that I may never lose the bliss of the touch of the one in the play of the many.[13]

*****
NOTES

1. Kripalani, Krishna, *Tagore, A Biography*, Grove Press, Inc, 1962, p. 398.

The closeness of Tagore's relationship to Gandhi is indicated in the following excerpt from the *Biography*, pp. 367 ff.

"On 20 September 1932 the whole nation was stunned by the news of Mahatma Gandhi in jail resorting to a fast 'unto death.' At 3:00 a.m. of the day on which he was to begin the fast he wrote to Tagore: Dear Gurudev, this is early morning 3 o'clock of Tuesday. I enter this fiery gate at noon. If you can bless the effort, I want it. You have been to me a true friend because you have been a candid friend often speaking your thoughts aloud. I had looked toward a firm opinion from you one way or the other. But you have refused to criticize. Though it can now be only during my fast, I will yet prize your criticism, if your heart condemns my action, I am not too proud to make an open confession, if I find myself in error. If your heart approves of the action I want your blessing. It will sustain me. I hope I have made myself clear.' At 10:00 a.m. he added a postscript to the above: "Just as I was handing this to the Superintendent, I got your loving and magnificent wire. It will sustain me in the midst of the storm I am about to enter. I am sending you a wire. Thank you."

"On 24 September Tagore, unable to keep himself away, left for Poona to visit the Mahatma in Yeravda Jail. The British government having conceded the demand and accepted the compromise proposed by all the political parties and communities in the country, the Mahatma broke his fast on the 26th, Tagore being present by his bedside in the jail. 'The fast taken in the name of God,' said the Mahatma in a public statement, 'was broken in His name in the presence of Gurudev [Tagore]. The breaking was preceded by the poet singing one of his Bengali hymns.' The hymn sung was the original of the *Gitanjali* poem:

*When the heart is hard and parched up, come upon me with
a shower of mercy.
When grace is lost from life, come with a burst of song.
When tumultuous work raised its din on all sides shutting
me out from beyond, come to me, my lord of silence, with
thy peace and rest.
When my beggarly heart sits crouched, shut up in a corner,
break open the door, my king, and come with the ceremony
of a king.
When desire blinds the mind with delusion and dust,
O thou holy one, thou wakeful, come with thy light and thy
thunder.* (Song 39)

2. Erik H. Erikson, *Gandhi's Truth, On the Origins of Militant Non-violence*, W.W. Norton and Co. Inc., N.Y, 1960.

3. Rabindranath Tagore, *Gitanjali*, International Pocket Library, Song 36, p. 27.

4. *Tagore—A Biography*, p. 249.

5. *Idem* p. 358.

6. *Idem* p. 387.

7. *Idem* p. 386.

8. *Idem* p. 361.

9. *Idem* p. 398.

10. *Idem* p. 249.

11. *Idem* p. 390.

12. *Idem* p. 392.

13. Tagore's *Gitanjali*, Song 63, p. 14.

REFLECTIONS ON RABINDRANATH TAGORE'S "GITANJALI" IV

When the heart is hard and parched up, come upon me with a shower of mercy.

When grace is lost from life, come with a burst of song. When tumultuous work raised its din on all sides shutting me out from beyond, come to me, my lord of silence, with thy peace and rest.

When my beggarly heart sits crouched, shut up in a corner, break open the door, my king, and come with the ceremony of a king.

When desire blinds the mind with delusion and dust,

O thou holy one, thou wakeful, come with thy light and thy thunder.[1]

Krishna Kripalani in his biography of Tagore[2] describes how this beautiful song was sung in 1932 in historic circumstances. The occasion was the breaking of a fast by Mahatma Gandhi—a fast which he had undertaken "unto death" in the struggle for Indian independence. The place was the Yeravada Jail. The fast was successful. Tagore was at Gandhi' side when the fast was broken. Gandhi made the following statement to the Indian people: "The fast taken in the name of God was broken in his name in the presence of Gurudev (Tagore)."

The breaking of the fast was preceded by an act of thanksgiving in which Tagore, sitting with Gandhi in the Yeravada Jail, sang the song I have just quoted.

The singing of the song under these circumstances illustrates the deep mutual respect and affection which bound Gandhi and Tagore together. It also is illustrative of the importance of songs and singing in revolutionary movements. When I think of this incident I think of small black children singing in the streets of Selma, "ain't nobody goin' turn me round - turn me round - turn me round." And I think of a march held last winter in Charleston, South Carolina when ten thousand of us, supporting some striking black hospital workers, went through the streets of Charleston singing a great variety of freedom songs, among them the song so much associated with Martin Luther King, "Black and white together, we shall overcome."

Revolutions can be judged at one level by the character of the songs which the revolutionaries sing. They can also be judged in a measure by the character of the poets who write the songs.

As a poet and singer of songs, Tagore was very close to the aspirations of those leaders who led the struggle for Indian independence. He was particularly close to Gandhi, as illustrated by the incident at the Yeravada Jail.

The songs which he wrote and sang are by and large songs bringing out awareness of the need of the individual person for wholeness, for strength, for deeper identity. The images in the songs are religious. The setting of the songs is that of the entire cosmos, not that of narrow political dimensions, or nationalism. This is true even of songs which are primarily concerned with the ideal nation or the ideal society. For example, this very well-known prayer.

Where the mind is without fear and the head is held high;
Where knowledge is free;

Where the world has not broken up into fragments by narrow domestic walls;
Where tireless striving stretches its arm toward perfection;
Where the clear stream of reason has not lost its way into the dreary desert sand of dead habit;
Where the mind is led by thee into ever-widening thought and action —
Into that heaven of freedom, my Father, let my country awake.[3]

    This song is not a dilettante exercise in song writing, irrelevant to the issues of the struggle for independence then being waged. It was totally relevant then and is totally relevant now to the present struggle going on in our own country for justice for the blacks, for a redefinition of the meaning of patriotism, for the end of the Vietnam War, for radical change in our economy and our ideology both of which have become bloated with militarism. The song is an enduring plea for the right kind of pride, for intelligence, for reason, for faith in the future. It transcends the interests of any one party, of any one race, sect or nation. Its images are cosmopolitan.

    I read last week for the first time F.S.C. Northrop's *Essay on Tagore*.[4] Like everything of Northrop's that I have read, it is perceptive and provocative. At one point in the essay, after making a comment on the large and positive contribution made by Tagore to India's nationalism, Northrop goes on to make this comment:

"But Tagore's nationalism transcended all national boundaries, as did the spirit of his Buddhist Hinduism. Because his religious philosophy taught him that the deepest and real self in all persons, whether Buddhist Hindus or not, is, like the timeless pool or ocean in its relation to its transitorily different waves, the same in all mankind and even all cosmic creatures, Tagore envisaged the different religions and religious nations of the world as diverse, wave-like differentiations of the Divine self in all of us.

"This led him to seek out the deepest and best in all religions and religiously rooted peoples. Like India's present Vice President, Professor Radhakrishan, he realized that God is one, though the ways to Him be many. For clearly the Divine, which is timeless, indeterminate, and infinite, cannot be revealed in determinate, transitory, finite terms without being exhibited as but one manifestation of its infinite nature. Any nation or religion, consequently, which is to be true to the deepest nature of its own adherents, must behave similarly, in the same cosmopolitan and tolerant spirit, enriching its deepest understanding of its own self and provincial nation by seeing God's different, religiously political manifestations in other religious faiths and nations. This Tagore did for Islam as well as Buddhist-Hindu India, and for all the other religious civilizations and nations of the world as well."

I think that all of Tagore's songs come out of this kind of cosmic consciousness. and this kind of cosmic consciousness is much more real to us today - particularly to young people - than it was thirty years ago. I think this is one of the reasons why Buddhist and Hindu teachers are listened to with so much respect by so many young people. I suspect it is the reason why persons like Tagore and Gandhi will, so to speak, come back to play a larger role in the shaping of religious thought and attitudes in the future in the west than they have in the past. This, as I see it, is also one reason why Tagore's *Song Offerings* is only at the beginning of its influence. Its cosmopolitan character will commend it to a generation whose emphasis is increasingly on universals. Its appeal to the person will constantly commend it to those who are tired of abstractions, collectivizations and mass appeals of all kinds. The concreteness of its images, their naturalness—not to mention the qualities of beauty and imagination—will appeal to those who shy away from tired-out language, the language which was appropriate to saints and mystics indulging the thought categories of the medieval period but which lacks contemporary breadth of thought and feeling.

Those of us who know these songs and love them have no difficulty in appreciating the truth of W.B. Yeats' statement of what they mean to him:

> "I have carried the manuscript of these translations about with me for days, reading it in railway trains, or on the tops of omnibuses and in restaurants, and I have often had to close it lest some stranger would see how much it moved me. These lyrics—which are in the original, my Indians tell me, full of subtlety of rhythm, of untranslatable delicacies of colour, of metrical invention—display in their thought a world I have dreamed of all my life long. The work of a supreme culture, they yet appear as much the growth of the common soil as the grass and the rushes. A tradition, where poetry and religion are the same thing, has passed through the centuries, gathering from learned and unlearned metaphor and emotion, and carried back again to the multitude the thought of the scholar and of the noble."[5]

Tagore's social concern comes out of cosmic consciousness and today the mood runs increasingly toward cosmic consciousness.

Tagore has a God-awareness that goes beyond any final expression but is always at the heart of his experience. It always shines through the metaphors and images of his songs.

Many of us have lost the capacity to use the word "God" without extreme self-consciousness. We are trapped in the literal character of our own thought habits. It takes a poet to break us loose and shake us loose. In the songs of Tagore God becomes all the realities which are most meaningful and precious to us: the man playing a flute in a boat on a river, my friend the beloved. God is as real as flowers and rivers, the blowing of conch shells, the parching heat.[6] The experience of God-awareness is one with our awareness of the reality of joy and sorrow, beauty and ugliness in the world about us. The Divine is present in play and in work, in silence and music, in steps on a road outside a house, in the openness of sky, in the infinite variety of moods that sweep over the human spirit.

In all the songs of Tagore the underlying theme is the reality of the Divine, the reality of stratagems by which we cut ourselves off from the Divine, and the reality of the experience by which the Divine manifests itself in the common day.

Of course, the songs speak best for themselves. Consider these songs picked more or less at random, illustrative of the point:

He whom I enclose with my name is weeping in this dungeon. I am ever busy building this wall all around; and as this wall goes up into the sky day by day I lose sight of my true being in its dark shadow.

I take pride in this great wall, and I plaster it with dust and sand lest a least hole should be left in this name; and for all the care I take I lose sight of my true being.[7]

Art thou abroad on this stormy night on the journey of love, my friend? The sky groans like one in despair.

I have no sleep tonight. Ever and again I open my door and look out on the darkness, my friend!

I can see nothing before me. I wonder where lies thy path!

By what dim shore of the ink-black river, by what far edge of the frowning forest, through what mazy depth of gloom art thou threading thy course to come to me, my friend?[8]

I ask for a moment's indulgence to sit by thy side. The words that I have in hand I will finish afterwards.

Away from the sight of thy face my heart knows no rest nor respite, and my work becomes an endless toil in a shoreless sea of toil.

Today the summer has come at my window with its sighs and murmurs; and the bees are plying their minstrelsy at the court of the flowering grove.

Now it is time to sit quiet, face to face with thee, and to sing dedication of life in this silent and overflowing leisure.[9]

In these songs God-awareness is itself the ultimate reality, the source of life, the source of song. It needs no justification, though being human we ask for justification. We are anxious and we worry, but when we ask for justification we are given more songs. And they are songs which refer to that which is not to be proved or disproved. Do we worry about lost time? The poet sings:

On many an idle day have I grieved over lost time. But it is never lost, my lord. Thou has taken every moment of my life in thine own hands.

Hidden in the heart of things thou are nourishing seeds into sprouts, buds into blossoms, and ripening flowers into fruitfulness.

I was tired and sleeping on my idle bed and imagined all work had ceased. In the morning I woke up and found my garden full of wonders of flowers.

Do we worry that at the end of the day there will be no time? The poet sings that at the end of the day and at the end of all days there will still be time.

Time is endless in thy hands, my lord. There is none to count thy minutes.

Days and nights pass and ages bloom and fade like flowers. Thou knowest how to wait.

Thy centuries follow each other perfecting a small wild flower.

We have no time to lose, and having to time we must scramble for our chances. We are too poor to be late.

And thus it is that time goes by while I give it to every querulous man who claims it, and thine altar is empty of all offerings to the last.

At the end of the day I hasten in fear lest thy gate be shut; but I find that yet there is time.[11]

And yet there is in these songs no moving away from the moving stream of life in which our lives intermingle, no snug, secure view of life. There is a quality of poignancy and sadness which all of us experience, but this quality, too, like everything else the poet touches is caught up in a song of great beauty. And in this song, as in all of Tagore's songs, no circle is drawn around the mystery. It remains a source of wonder.

On the seashore of endless worlds children meet. The infinite sky is motionless overhead and the restless water is boisterous. On the seashore of endless worlds the children meet with shouts and dances.

They build their houses with sand and they play with empty shells. With withered leaves they weave their boats and smilingly float them on the vast deep. Children have their play on the seashore of worlds.

They know not how to swim, they know not how to cast nets. Pearl fishers dive for pearls, merchants sail in their ships, while children gather pebbles and scatter them again. They seek not for hidden treasures, they know not how to cast net.

The sea surges up with laughter and pale gleams the smile of the sea beach. Death-dealing waves sing meaningless ballads to the children, even like a mother while rocking her baby's cradle. The sea plays with children, and pale gleams the smile of the sea beach.

On the seashore of endless worlds children meet. Tempest roams in the pathless sky, ships get wrecked in the trackless waters, death is abroad and children play. On the seashore of endless worlds is the great meeting of children.[12]

The poet lives the poignancy, the wonder and the sadness. In his own way, he finds within himself Camus' "invincible summer" and in his own words he sings it.

I thought my voyage had come to its end at the last limit of my power—that the path before me was closed, that provisions were exhausted and the time come to take shelter in silent obscurity.

But I find that thy will knows no end in me. And when old worlds die out on the tongue, new melodies break forth from the heart; and where the old tracks are lost, new country is revealed with its wonders.[13]

And such song of wonder, joy and thanksgiving as this one:

Thou has made me known to friends whom I knew not. Thou hast given me seats in homes not my own. Thou has brought the distant near and made a brother of the stranger.

I am uneasy at heart when I have to leave my accustomed shelter; I forget that there abides the old in the new and that there also thou abidest.

Through birth and death, in this world or in others, wherever thou leadest me it is thou, the same, the one companion of my endless life who ever linkest my heart with bonds of joy to the unfamiliar.

When one knows thee, then alien there is none, then no door is shut. Oh, grant me my prayer that I many never lose the bliss of the touch of the one in the play of the many.[14]

*****

NOTES

1. Tagore's *Gitanjali*, Song 39, p. 28 (International Pocket Library).

2. Tagore, A Biography, p. 366 ff (Kripalani, Krishna, Grove Press Inc., 1962).

3. Tagore's *Gitanjali*, Song 35, p. 26.

4. F.S.C. Northrop, *Man, Nature and God, A Quest for Life's Meaning*, Pocket Books, Inc., New York, 1962, p. 181.

5. Tagore's *Gitanjali*, pp. 7 & 8.

6. Tagore's *Gitanjali*, p. 9.

7. Tagore's *Gitanjali*, Song 29, p. 24.

8. Tagore's *Gitanjali*, Song 23, p. 22.

9. Tagore's *Gitanjali*, Song 5, p. 14.

10. Tagore's *Gitanjali*, Song 81, p. 51.

11. Tagore's *Gitanjali*, Song 82, p. 51.

12. Tagore's *Gitanjali*, Song 60, p. 40.

13. Tagore's *Gitanjali*, Song 37, p. 27.

14. Tagore's *Gitanjali*, Song 63, p. 42.

THE FLOWERING OF THE SPIRIT

I should like to speak this morning on a phrase from a poem by Stephen Spender. If I am accurate in my memory, this poem was written *in memoriam* to those British airmen who lost their lives in the Battle of Britain. I read only a portion of the poem:

What is precious is never to forget
The delight of the blood drawn from ageless springs
Breaking through rocks in worlds before our earth;
Never to deny its pleasure in the simple morning light,
Nor its grave evening demand for love;
Never to allow gradually the traffic to smother
With noise and fog the flowering of the spirit.

I am an old hand myself at writing sermons, and in the process I am used to discovering in myself resistances without end. Yet I was surprised at the resistance I discovered within myself in speaking to this theme. I have learned also not only to discover resistances but sometimes to ask myself why I am so resistant. And there are, of course, as any person who speaks in public a good deal will recognize, many causes. Sometimes the cause is simply physical weariness. Caught up in a welter of such varied tasks, with so many demands—central and extraneous—on one's time, the energy runs out; and one tries to lift up an idea when he has not the strength to get if off the ground.

It may be that a speaker is trying to talk about something that is not rightfully his. I always recall in this connection the wisdom of David, who, when he was going to fight Goliath, was given a chance by Saul, the king, to wear his great armor. David looked at it, no doubt with a great desire to wear it—he would have liked to have a photograph taken and sent home—but he realized it was not his armor. He took his own native weapons—stones from the creek, and a sling. This is the reason, really, why he won his battle over Goliath: that he was willing to fight Goliath with his own weapons and not assay to use someone else's. So it may be that I am trying to say something that does not belong to me. That causes great difficulty.

Or it may be that I am trying to expose myself in a way that I am not yet ready to do. "I'll have to wait awhile," I tell myself, "before I can tell you that much about myself." The image that comes to mind, for some reason, is the picture of a fallen log over a fast-moving stream. We stand at one end of the log, hesitantly, realizing how slippery the log looks and how wet the water; questioning seriously whether this is our day to walk over such a slippery log.

it may be that I am trying to expose myself in a way that I am not yet ready to do

It was apparent, as soon as I began working at this theme, that the phrase "the flowering of the spirit" caused my great uneasiness. As I came up against it and then walked away from it, I became aware of an ambivalence that made me confess I was afraid of it at the same time I was attracted to it. Before I could do anything else, I had to ask myself the grounds of my ambivalence; and having asked, I could then go on to think a bit about the intrinsic meaning of the phrase itself.

What was the ground of the ambivalence?—I am sure that it is not a ground on which I walk alone. What is the content of the saying? What does the phrase mean—"the flowering of the spirit"? What does it mean to you?

On the one hand, I can identify it with certain personality or character qualities of a positive kind. When these qualities are an integral part of our characters, we are authentic. We are whole in our ways of sorrowing and rejoicing, in our ways of loving and hating, and in our ways to trusting and doubting. We say of such authentic persons—and we all know at least a few of them, and we have all been such persons, and are such persons at certain points in our living—we say, "He is a real person. When I am with him there is a communication between us that defies articulation. There is a sense of the Presence. I gain strength, warmth, wholeness, authenticity, realness. When I am with him, I know that I am a real person too."

When these qualities are an integral part of our characters, we are authentic

This is one way of talking about the flowering of the spirit. But the question which I find myself asking about this quality of wholeness or holiness—the two words come from the same root—is this: If this is the flowering of the spirit, to what shall we relate it? From whence does it spring? Shall we regard it as an autonomous phenomenon, the manifestation of superbly human qualities created by a person in his own life? Or shall we regard it as a manifestation in human life of a spirit which runs through all things?

I found that as I tried to understand my ambivalence, two desires came together like streams of water flowing against one another. The one was the desire to believe that the flowering of the spirit has to be set in the context of human autonomy. It arises out of the life of some individual, some person or some group. It is controlled by some person or some group. We create it. We cultivate it. We nourish it. And that is all that need be said about it. It is our plant and we sow it, we reap it.

But there was another voice in me which said, *Not so*. This is simply not true. When we speak of this flowering of the spirit, we are talking of an autonomous person, true, but not of an autonomous person alone. We are talking of a mutuality which holds all things together. We are talking of a process which binds together all things and which can never be explained or understood in terms of human autonomy alone. We are talking of a reality which, in a measure, transcends the individual and the race, and is the product, as it were, of many and strange worlds interacting one upon another. Thus when the flowering of the spirit takes place in us, there is present in us aspects of a universal life. We cannot, in any exclusive sense, take the credit for it finally, because the credit does not belong to us.

Here was a conflict in me which was as much psychological as theological. As I thought about this conflict, sayings from different ages and in different idioms began to rise from my memory.

From the 139th Psalm:

Whither shall I go from thy spirit? or whither shall I flee from they presence?

If I ascend up into heaven, thou art there: if I make my bed in hell, behold, thou art there.

If I take the wings of the morning, and dwell in the uttermost parts of the sea;

Even there shall thy hand lead me, and thy right hand shall hold me.

That is a passage that goes way back in the history of religious literature.

Emerson's essay on the *Over-Soul*:

"Man is a stream whose source is hidden. Our being is descending into us from we know not whence. The most exact calculator has no prescience that somewhat incalculable may not balk at the next moment. [And then this phrase, which I have not been able to forget since I read it first in college.] I am constrained every moment to acknowledge a higher origin for events than the will I call mine."

These recollections, you may say, are from thinkers from the past. What about the present? I think of words of Lewis Mumford which I read perhaps twenty-four years ago, when his *Faith for Living* was first published. These words, Mumford wrote, are the basis not only for personal living but are the basis ultimately for all social living or social action.

> "Men are individually nothing except in relation to that greater reality, Man. And Man himself is nought except in relation to that greater reality which he calls divine. Thought, art, love are all intimations of this divinity: flickering of man-made filaments that connect, in our imaginations, with distant flashes in the dark impenetrable sky."[1]

Or I think of the words of a contemporary biologist. I don't know N.J. Berrill's writings in their entirety, but certain passages of his that I have read seem to strike a kindling flame.

> "Life had a very long and a very diversified history on this planet before we emerged and no one has guaranteed us our right to possession—we could be a passing whim of creation fading away as imperceptibly as we had began, with no one to mourn us or to realize that we had ever been. And unless we had irrevocably poisoned the planet with radioactive waste (I see by the morning paper that scientists have discovered in some distant sea a radioactive whale that has absorbed in its body these poisons which we have spread.) during our incumbency the world would roll on around its sun without us, wonderfully rich and beautiful, incessantly evolving new forms of life on land and in the sea and in the air. Color and scent and sound would still be sensed by other creatures. Birds would still sing for joy, flowers would still grow in season, and other mammals might evolve a large though different sort of brain more consciously earthborn and earthbound than ours. Beauty would remain, to be sought and to be seen. Yet it would be a shame to falter and step aside when we have

some so far; for if the fertility of a planet is life and the fruit of life is mind, then the human species becomes the first sign of real wakefulness in the solar system. And this I believe is our true meaning and significance."[2]

This is a fresh way of thinking about ancient questions. I wonder when I read this kind of description of man whether or not the twentieth-century biologist is not trying to say something akin to what was said by the ancient writer of the Book of Proverbs: "The spirit of man is the candle of the Lord"—"The human species is the first sign of the wakefulness of the solar system."

Speaking now not only of the arguments which I encountered in the composition of this sermon, but speaking from personal experience, my ambivalence seems to be giving way before my awareness that my own growth, my own flowering as a person, or your growth, your flowering as persons, is always part of a larger process. This process catches up in its wake vitalities and mysteries which no single person, no single life, and perhaps no single world can encompass. Our individual lives always have to be seen as part of the flowering of a wider context of life. We encounter worlds within worlds. We encounter universes flowing out of universes. The little world of "I" and "me" cannot be understood unless it is set like a jewel in the midst of a mystery. We can prove with our intellects here and there—and we should never discount the importance of this probing—but intellectually, as someone has said, we stand on an island in the midst of an illimitable ocean of inexplicability. In every generation we seek to reclaim a little more land, to add something to the extent and solidarity of what we call, probably erroneously, "our possessions." We mirror our universe. We are our universe. Our universe is held together by that which we do not understand, but the Presence we feel is very real.

> *my ambivalence seems to be giving way before my awareness*

I think of the poem, *The Hound of Heaven*, by Francis Thompson. We can say, in a rather bizarre extension of Thompson's metaphor, that the universe we live in is a ball held in the mouth of a divine dog.[3]

There comes to mind finally a passage from the writings of the distinguished anthropologist, Loren Eiseley, found in his John Dewey Lecture. This is a passage worth pondering:

> "When I was a small boy I lived, more than most children, in two worlds. One was dark, hidden and self-examining, though in its own way not without compensations. The other world in which I somehow also managed to exist was external, boisterous, and what I suppose the average parent would call normal or extroverted. These two worlds simultaneously existing in one growing brain had in them something of the dichotomy present in the actual universe where one finds behind the ridiculous, wonderful tentshow of woodpeckers, giraffes, and hoptoads, some kind of dark, brooding, but creative void out of which these things emerge—some anti-matter universe, some web of dark tensions running beneath and creating the superficial show of form that so delights us. If I develop this little story or a personal experience as a kind of parable, it is because I believe that in one way or another we mirror in ourselves the universe with all its dark vacuity and also its simultaneous urge to create anew, in each generation, the beauty and the terror of our mortal existence."[4]

We mirror the universe with its dark vacuity, its dark emptiness, on the one hand. On the other we mirror the simultaneous urge of the universe to create anew in each generation the beauty and the terror of our mortal existence.[5]

Whatever the diligence, whatever the courage, whatever the steadfastness of the imagination with which we cultivate our own gardens in our own time and in our own way, the flowering of the spirit is a part of a creativity which is both within us and beyond us.

What is precious is never to forget
The delight of the blood drawn from ageless springs
Breaking through rocks in worlds before our earth;
Never to deny its pleasure in the simple morning light,
Nor its grave evening demand for love;
Never to allow gradually the traffic to smother
With noise and fog the flowering of the spirit.

*****

NOTES

1. Lewis Mumford, *Faith for Living*, Harcourt, Brace and Company, New York, 1940, p. 210.

2. N. J. Berrill, *Man's Emerging Mind*, Premier Books (Fawcett World Library), New York, 1957, p. 210 (Originally published by Dodd, Mead & Co.).

3. This thought was probably suggested to me by a passage from a poem by Kaye Dunham as well as by Francis' Thompson's well-known poem:

I tell you
I tell you
I tell you
This world is a
Wereless world
In the mouth of the
Nameless God
Seek him.

The quiet candle
Flame and
The shattering thunder
Quake
Both do gently
Lead me to that
Delicate Meeting
Place
And thee.

4. Loren Eiseley, *The Mind as Nature,* Harper & Row, New York and Evanston, 1962, pp. 17,18.

THE NEED FOR NON-VIOLENT DISSENT IN THE STREETS

On November 2, 1969 the following letter appeared in The New York *Times*:

PEACE DEMONSTRATORS

"To the Editor:

After all the years of war, it is a sad fact that voices in the United States continue to cry that peace demonstrations either aid Hanoi, prolong the war, or are placing the knife in the backs of American soldiers or desecrating their graves.

The ignoble way in which we stumbled into a major war, as well as the revulsion of scores of millions to this war are facts of life. Policy makers ignore such data at their peril (ours also); when they do, blood is on their hands. Ambassador Harriman justly warned that the American body politic must act according to stronger impulses than fear of the Communist propaganda mill.

We in Vietnam have as much support as we need. I, for one, would sleep more soundly if I didn't have to read or hear about officials and would-be officials who slander their countrymen, who feel it is self-evident that dissenters must be subversives or dupes. Evidently, the lessons of the free society are yet to be learned by some of its most avid defenders.

(Capt.) Jason R. Gettinger
Vietnam, Oct. 21, 1969"

This is a good take-off point for further thought on the controversy being carried on across the country. I agree with Jason Gettinger. I think there is something un-American and, if I may use the word, *subversive*, in appeals for muffling or withholding criticism on the issue of the Vietnam War; in the appeal that we muffle our criticism of President Nixon as he seeks to implement his Vietnam War policy.

The Vietnam War has gone on too long already and has cost too much. Following are some statistics, official Department of Defense figures, which give us some idea of the cost. In 1968 14,500 Americans died in Vietnam. As of October 15, 11,000 had died in the current calendar year. As of September 1969 the total of the American dead was 44,798. The total South Vietnamese dead was 93,738. The total North Vietnamese and National Liberation Front dead was 546,804. The total dead in all the armed services in the war is approximately 700,000. I say nothing of the wounded. I say nothing of the civilian dead, displaced, sick, impoverished, tortured.

By 1970 the United States will have spent a hundred ten billion dollars on this war. This is ten times the total amount spent on Medicare, fourteen times the amount spent on all levels of support for education and some fifty times the amount spent on housing and community development during the same period.

Arthur Schlesinger, Jr. quotes I.F. Stone on the bombing of Vietnam:

"The total bomb tonnage dropped on Vietnam, North and South, through October 1968, was 2,948,057 tons. The total tonnage dropped during the second world war in both the

European and Pacific theaters was 2,057,244 tons. This means that the American planes dropped almost 50 percent more tons of explosives on this hapless country than were dropped on Japan, Germany, and the other enemy territories during the last world war."

We should remember that no president of the United States has been immune to criticism. In totalitarian countries one criticizes the leader at grave peril, and one publicly criticizes governmental policy at his peril. This is true of all kinds of dictatorships and oligarchies from the Soviet Union, to Egypt, to South Vietnam, and I suppose to North Vietnam. Public criticism is risky and public demonstrations so far out of the question as to be hardly the subject of fantasy!

no president of the United States has been immune to criticism

Charles Beard writes that one of the greatest moments in our history came during the Civil War when, despite the existence of a terrible civil war, an election for the presidency was held. He regards this fact as one of the greatest achievements of our society.

In our country, as I have said, no president has ever been exempt from blunt criticism—not even George Washington. Several years ago I had the opportunity to read a 2-volume study of the life of Jefferson and his times. One of the aspects of the times which particularly impressed me was the radical and outspoken nature of controversies which distinguished our country in that early period. Indeed, I remember thinking it was a miracle that a young country could hold together in the face of such controversy and such radical differences of conviction.

To argue in the name of unity, patriotism, and victory that criticism should be muted at this time is to argue that we are now so weak, or in such peril that a peculiar kind of sanctuary should be given to the present occupant of the White House and to the present policies of the government. I think it would be really unpatriotic and dangerous to suspend criticism and to try to muffle strident voices under the rubric of "Let's all pull together for victory." The argument that unity is that important ignores the facts of life. It ignores the truth that when our country is in a time of crisis and great transition, an essential resource to help it through the crisis is controversy. An essential test of its health is its capacity to withstand and utilize the tensions generated by strong debates. It ignores the fact that it is out of these tensions that fresh solutions can arise to meet complex problems. Remember those words of Abraham Lincoln spoken at a time of crisis in 1865, "The dogmas of the quiet past are inadequate to the stormy present. The occasion is piled high with difficulty, and we must rise with the occasion. As our case is new, we must think anew and act anew. We must disenthrall ourselves." This is an invitation of new thought, radical thought, not an attempt to cut off debate and proceed in our national life along traditional lines.

I think there are many who would agree with me completely up to this point, but would then go on to say that tensions and disagreements are all right so long as they are kept in the halls of Congress, in schools, in universities, in churches and in forums of a conventional outdoor variety. Controversies are all right indoors, they would say, but they must be kept indoors, in conventional channels and off the streets. Why? The answer seems to be—and I have discussed this with many people right here in our own church—that public demonstrations, peace marches, peace walks, all varieties of demonstrations in the streets are emotional appeals which are divisive and could lead to violence.

All this is perfectly true. I have participated in a good many public demonstrations of one kind or another. Certainly there exists in all of them in varying degrees considerable emotion and even the threat of violence. The extent to which the threat of violence is present varies widely. Sometimes it is virtually non-existent, as in some of the peace rallies we held here in San Francisco eight or nine years ago protesting nuclear testing. Sometimes a public demonstration is a virtual tinderbox, as at Selma, Alabama, when hostile armed deputies faced determined and committed people from out of state. The contempt, hatred and fear on the faces of the deputies was too strong to be denied. San Francisco State College last year found the students and the police at a highly combustible stage of meeting. We should remember, however, that when violence breaks out, indiscriminate violence, the police who are trained to deal with unruly crowds bear a heavier share of responsibility for restraint than can be assigned to those who are being policed. The police in London have shown us how well-trained police forces can cope with great masses of people in an effective and restrained manner. Some of the peace demonstrations in which I have taken part have been amazing models of restraint and non-violence on the part of thousands of people. The great rally in Washington, D.C. in November of 1965 was one of these. Several of the great rallies protesting the Vietnamese War here in San Francisco have been similarly examples of great restraint and dignity. But in mass demonstrations the potential for violence is always there, and many of us who have been active demonstrators can recall uneasy moments when the specter of violence appeared very real.

There is a point at which there may be such a massive threat of violence that the constitutional guarantees of freedom of assembly and speech might have to be suspended. But that point is far from being reached or even approached at the present time.

Those who assume that the planned demonstrations for the coming weekend should be curbed because of the threat of violence are guilty of hysteria.

They may be guilty of something else which is more dangerous than hysteria, and that is the cynical desire to discredit the peace marchers by exaggerating the danger of violence. They may even be guilty of the desire for violence which, once it had broken out, could be used by them as a pretest for crippling the peace movement.

I am in complete agreement with the contention of Dr. Benjamin Spock and Mrs. Martin Luther King that in its effort to deny the right of peace marchers to march down Pennsylvania Avenue in Washington, D.C. next weekend, the government is exaggerating the possibility of violence in order to keep people away and weaken the demonstration.

At Washington, D.C. there will be from three to six thousand volunteer marshals along the line of march to keep order. The most prominent citizens who have endorsed and will participate in the march, persons like William Sloane Coffin, chaplain of Yale University, Mrs. Martin Luther King, Dr. Benjamin Spock are making every effort to underscore the fact that violence is completely contrary to the purposes of the march and they, with their enormous moral prestige and influence will do everything they can to see that this gigantic witness for peace will be carried on in the tradition of non-violence.

But if there should be violence, it becomes all the more important to those of us who are committed to non-violent modes of protest that we be in the line of march. We should accept the responsibility to make the non-violent character of the protest unequivocally clear.

There are many reasons why I shall be marching here in San Francisco on Saturday. I hope that there will be large numbers of our congregation on the streets. I am glad to offer some of my reasons for taking part in this witness.

In the first place, I believe that we have to witness in the streets to something that did not even come into the President's speech last Monday night.[1] We have to show citizens in our country and throughout the world that there are those of us who are humiliated and shamed that we should ever have gotten into Vietnam in the first place. I remember very shortly after the Gulf of Tonkin Resolution was passed in the Senate I said in a sermon that the action of the Johnson Administration was a major tragedy, that we would find to our sorrow that it was much easier to put hundreds or thousands of soldiers on the Asian continent than it would be to take them off that continent. We should march to show that we feel that there is no honor in Vietnam for us. This is a dishonorable war. There was no honor in going in. There will be no honor in getting out, except as our withdrawal and the total sad lesson of Vietnam helps us to shift our national priority from war to peace. At the present time we are sick unto death with militarism.

At the present time we are sick unto death with militarism

In the second place, irrespective of whether 77%[2] or 97% of those who heard the speech approved of it, we must show that there are many people in this country willing to witness for different kinds of American vision than that which President Nixon's leadership is reflecting. We have a duty to make it very clear that our country is indeed divided on this issue. It would be a sad day, indeed, if the rest of the world were to think that we were all behind our Vietnam policy.

In the third place, it is important that demonstrations embrace the widest variety of segments of the American community. We need a tremendous cross-section of Americans, young citizens and old citizens, the hippy and the straight, the students and those who have long since been out of school. Currently there is a lot of talk among us about the silent majority. It is part of a vital democracy and the silent majority needs to come to terms with the thinking of a concerned and dedicated minority which will not be silenced. History tells us how very often the deeper insights, the more healing truths have come into the world and have been kept alight in the world and sustained in the world by a minority which saw more clearly than the majority where the truth was and what must be done about it.

In the fourth place, there is another way of being concerned about this issue of violence. I believe that unless our national policies are changed, and changed rapidly, there is likely to be violence. The longer we stay in Vietnam, the longer we continue to follow present militaristic policies, the more likely is the danger of violence—

radical violence—which will destroy our democratic institutions and cause us to lose faith in the workability of democratic ideals.

In the fifth place, there is a real practical reason for these demonstrations in the streets. We cannot command a half-hour or forty minutes of prime television time simply for the asking of it as the President of the United States can. Our presence is felt as we are seen on the streets in the largest possible numbers with the greatest possible dignity—dignity and non-violent witnessing. I do not know how many of you did participate in the October 15th witness here in San Francisco. The people I saw on Union Square and before the Federal Building on that day did not come across to me as "impudent snobs" or "effete intellectuals." They came across as deeply concerned fellow-Americans, concerned enough about their children, their country, the fate of their world, the fate of soldiers and civilians dying in Vietnam, the ills of society sick to death with war—concerned enough about all these things to walk, sing, march in the rain to bear a solemn, but at times, a joyful pubic witness.

I remember one incident on October 15 which was dramatic precisely because it was not dramatic. I stood for quite a long time with a small group of people, seven to ten of them, standing in the rain singing together in a simple, melodic chant, these words: "All we are saying is—give peace a chance." I must admit that I sang with this group and looked up at the Federal Building towering above us, symbol of big government, great power, and found myself asking of this small group could possibly have any influence in the short or long run. But they influenced me, and they reinforced my conviction as to the importance of that kind of witness. If they influenced me, they influenced others. It is not easy to say where moral influence begins and once it starts it is difficult to raise barriers that can wipe it out.

These people and their fellow citizens singing in the rain were seeking to restore us to the better part of our heritage, to rekindle the vision which is the better part of America,

I began this morning by reading a letter from Capt. Jason R. Gettinger, currently stationed in Vietnam. I would conclude with some of his words which seem to me to go to the very heart of the matter:

"The ignoble way in which we stumbled into a major war, as well as the revulsion of scores of millions to this war are facts of life. Policy makers ignore such data at their peril (ours also); when they do, blood is on their hands. Ambassador Harriman justly warned that the American body politic must act according to stronger impulses than fear of the Communist propaganda mill."

We are an important part of that American body politic. We nurture a vision that our country can, in truth, be beautiful. It has been beautiful at times in the past and it will be beautiful again. But it can only be beautiful if it stands for peace. And it can only stand for peace if we ourselves speak the word with out feet and with our visible presence, as well as with our words. It can only be beautiful if we live the word peace so clearly, so resolutely, so imaginatively that there is no way in which any person in our country can escape its vibrations.

CLOSING WORDS

Here lies our tragedy
Not that we are fearful,
Men have always lived with fear.
Not that we are wicked,
Who can claim to be perfectly good?
But that we are stranger,
Too slow to perceive our common kinship
Too slow to understand that truly we
are members one of another.

*****

NOTES

1. Speech of President Nixon on Vietnam given Monday evening, November 3, 1969.

2. Gallup Poll findings presented in newspapers a day or two following the Nixon address showed that 77% of those Americans who heard it approved of it.

PEACE AND OUR BLINDNESS

Reflections on the Siege of Leningrad

On June 19, 1966, Mrs. Scholefield and I flew from London to Leningrad to be willing and enthusiastic celebrants of the White Nights Festival, which that year was dedicated to the genius of the composer, Dmitri Shostakovich. Our first night there, a Sunday night, we found a park just a few minutes walk from the hotel. It was a beautiful spring evening. We walked in the park for more than an hour. Men and boys were playing a variety of games: chess, checkers, dominoes and ping-pong. Men and women were strolling and reading. Families were walking through the park together. It was a sizable park, running along a canal. We noted that it was not kept in the meticulous, stylized fashion of the parks in Paris, or of Ruskin Park in the southeast section of London where we were living. It was "natural." And there was something natural, good and comforting in the attitudes and games and friendliness of the people enjoying it on that lovely Sunday evening.

During the nearly two weeks we spent in Leningrad that park came to play a real role in our lives. Early each morning I would walk in it before breakfast. At that time I was using Tagore's *Gitanjali*[1] for meditation purposes, and the park was a good setting for reflection *on* and memorization *of* those "song offerings." Somehow it became a window for me on the life and spirit of the city.

Also, I became interested in and friendly with a family of three crows which lived in the park. They used to perch on the roof of the Europa Hotel where we were staying. At that time of the year the nights are very short, hence the name of the Festival—"White Nights." And these three crows would sometimes sit on the ridge of the roof of the hotel very early in the morning, and make a variety of comments to one another. I was pleased with myself when I discovered their nest in the park, so that I would see and hear them—sometimes at the park and sometimes back at the hotel. I was somehow reassured to find that Communist crows do not appear to differ in any great way from corvus Americanus. I am sure that whatever problems we citizens of the U.S.A. and U.S.S.R. may have in getting along with each other, American and Soviet crows appear to have the wit and ingenuity to get beyond differing ideologies!

Those three crows came back into my mind a few days ago when I was reading Harrison Salisbury's story of the siege of Leningrad.[2] There is a passage in his book on the disappearance of the bird during the siege, and his description provoked memories and reflections. Here is the passage:

> "There were, of course, no more birds in Leningrad. First to disappear were the crows, the black-and-gray northern European crows. They flew off to the German lines in November. Next to go were the gulls and pigeons. Then the sparrows and starlings vanished. They died of cold and hunger just as the people did. Some said they had seen sparrows drop like stones while flying over the Neva, simply frozen to death in flight. An old ship worker, named Ilya Kroshin, recalled that when Petrograd was starving in 1920 the crows lived in the factory shops. "Now there are no crows," he observed sadly.[3]
>
> "There was hardly a cat or dog left in Leningrad by late December. They had all been eaten. But the trauma was great when a man came to butcher an animal which had lived on his affection for years. One elderly artist strangled his pet cat

and ate it, according to Vsevolod Vishnevsky. Later he tried to hang himself, but the rope failed, he fell to the floor, breaking his leg, and froze to death. The smallest Leningrad children grew up not knowing what cats and dogs were."

While in Leningrad I doubt that I had a thought to what had happened to the crows during the fantastic siege period in the city's history. And yet what happened to the birds and animals seems more comprehensible than what happened to the people. What happened to the population as a whole was so devastatingly catastrophic, so horrible that it beggars the imagination. Perhaps for the sake of our own feelings, we tend to block it out and to deny it as a place in our memory.

> *What happened to the population as a whole was so devastatingly catastrophic, so horrible that it beggars the imagination*

What happens to birds and animals in a city is a forecast to the way the winds are blowing. It may be a sign of impending tragedy, a warning of what we are ourselves doing to ourselves and our environment. As I recall Camus' novel *The Plague*, we are told, to begin with, of the finding of one dead rat. That one dead rat is the sign and symbol of the fate which is to overtake the city. By the way, this makes us recall the sea animals and birds recently washed ashore dead from the oil-polluted Santa Barbara Channel and its environs. What are these dead bodies saying to us?

Early in the Leningrad siege the birds deserted the city. The cats and dogs perished either through starvation or because they were eaten by starving people. The rats deserted the city to go to the front-lines outside the city for the soldiers were better fed—the soldiers had to be kept alive even if the civilians died. Recall the remark made by the American officer in Vietnam: "We had to destroy the village to save it." This is the crazy logic of war, the logic of the military side of ourselves. The rats went out to the trenches and fortifications of the soldiers, particularly to the fortifications of the German soldiers for they were the best fed ones.

I want to tell a story that Salisbury tells about a boy and a mouse. He gives us many vignettes of what happens in a great city starving to death. This one is one of the most poignant, but the poignancy is not bereft of hope.

"A mouse confronted one little Leningrad boy with a difficult moral problem. His grandmother had a tin box in which she put every scrap of bread and crackers. It was the family's 'iron reserves.' If all else failed—but only then—they would dig into the box. One day the boy was alone in the freezing flat. He heard a noise inside the tin can. He knew what this meant. A mouse was eating the iron reserves. He could not immediately decide what to do. Should he open the box and release the mouse? Should he open the box, kill the mouse and throw it away? Or should he kill the mouse and eat it? The last alternative was the one which most tempted him for, after all, the mouse had been consuming their food. But the thought of eating the mouse was repulsive. Finally, he took the lid from the box, shook it and let the mouse escape. After all, he thought, the mouse was as hungry as he, and how did he know whether it did not have as much right to live as he did?"[4]

This siege of a great and beautiful city filled with three million people which took place less than thirty years ago—how can we comprehend it? Here is a city so rich in art, the home of the Hermitage Museum, so rich in history, the home of the Czars, the birthplace of the Bolshevik Revolution—perhaps the most significant social revolution in modern history. How can we comprehend the magnitude of the suffering, the patience of the people, and their heroism? What is the relevance of the event to us?

It may be as C.P. Snow contends that the hard facts in the historical account of the siege speak more compellingly of its dimensions than any poem, novel or any other work of are can.[5]

In Leningrad we heard Shostakovitch's "Leningrad Symphony," played by the Leningrad Symphony Orchestra, written in the city during the siege. Certainly it spoke to us. But it still may be, as C.P. Snow contends, that ultimately it is the facts that describe the event most compellingly. Let us look at some of them.

The siege lasted 900 days, for many of which the city was encircled, except for an ice road across Lake Ladoga, by German troops. It lasted from June of 1941 to April of 1944. The first winter, the winter of 1941-42 was the coldest winter in thirty years. Death statistics cannot be considered precisely accurate because conditions in the city made absolute accuracy impossible, but the following picture is believed to be generally accurate. During the siege about a million persons left the city. Some eight hundred thousand died of starvation. The total deaths from all causes may have run as high as a million one hundred thousand.[6] Fifty-three thousand persons died in December of 1941. Estimates of deaths in January and February of 1942 range from three thousand five hundred to eight thousand daily. The total of deaths officially reported for the period December through February is 199,187. The official burying agency, The Funeral Trust, buried 89,968 bodies in March; 102,497 in April; and in May, 53,562. By the fall of 1942, Leningrad's population had been cut by more than 75%. This was due to evacuation as well as to starvation, though there must have been also many evacuees who died after being evacuated from the ravages of the siege.

> *eight hundred thousand died of starvation*

C.P. Snow, reviewing Salisbury's book, writes:[7]

"Three hundred fell at Thermopylae. No one knows, or can ever know the exact number of dead in the Leningrad siege, but it must be somewhere between 1,000,000 and 1,250,000. That is about the same as the entire losses the United States has suffered in war in the whole of its history, including the Civil War. This from a city whole population to start was about 3,000,000, approximately the size of greater Philadelphia. The sheer enormity of these figures has meant that we in the United States and the United Kingdom have never taken them into our imagination—any more than we have done with the total Russian dead in the Hitler war, almost 25,000,000 or more than one in ten of the national population."

What has all this to do with peace and our blindness?

There is a passage in Luke which has taken on increasing significance for me in these recent years.[8] I never go through the Easter-Passover season without reflecting on it, and Harrison Salisbury's book somehow makes the passage even more relevant this year. It is a passage telling of the grief which overwhelmed Jesus of Nazareth when in the last days of his life, he beheld the great city of Jerusalem and contemplated its eventual destruction:

> "And when he drew near and saw the city he wept over it, saying, would that even today you knew the things that make for peace! But now they are hid from your eyes. For the day shall come upon you, when your enemies will cast up a bank about you and surround you, and hem you in on every side and dash you to the ground, and your children with you, and they will not leave one stone upon another because you did not know the time of your visitation."

In our country we are blind to the magnitude of the sufferings of others

The New English Bible translates the last phrase, "because you did not know God's moment when it came."

Comparisons may be invidious and impossible. It is hard to say whether we are more or less enlightened as peace-seekers than the men and women of Jerusalem were two thousand years ago. I think we are, but the increase in enlightenment may have been more than canceled out by the immense growth in our self-destruction potential. Whatever comparisons might indicate, there is great blindness in us today. I see it manifesting itself in several ways.

In our country we are blind to the magnitude of the sufferings of others, particularly the magnitude of the suffering of the Soviet peoples during the II World War and the magnitude of the sufferings of the Vietnamese people inflicted on them by our intervention in their civil war. This blindness makes it impossible for us to understand the fears which bulk so large in Soviet thinking. It makes it hard for us to understand the hatred and fear which the North Vietnamese cherish against us.[9] We are blinded by our own affluence and by our own lack of suffering, comparatively speaking.

We are curiously blind, also, to our country's vulnerability to nuclear destruction or destruction through chemical and biological warfare, curiously blind to the fragile quality of our cities. They look so strong and durable—they are actually so fragile and ephemeral.[10]

In the British Museum there is a magnificent series of bas-relief murals, some three thousand years old, showing an ancient army storming a city. The warriors are swimming across a stream, perhaps a moat, and some of them are staying afloat by clinging to the inflated bladders of animals. Many times when I was using the Reading Room of the British Museum, I would leave my books and look at different things in the Museum, and this exhibit was one that fascinated me. Now it occurs to me that a more radical difference has evolved between storming a city in 1941-44 and the current year, than evolved in all the years from the days of the Assyrians to the storming of Leningrad. Hitler had given orders[11] that the population of Leningrad was to be exterminated, that the capitulation of the city was not to be accepted. But today this would be unnecessary. A Hitler now would need only order the firing of nuclear missiles from points any hundreds of miles distant to wipe out the population entirely. But we refuse to face the revolutionary nature of changes in modern warfare brought about by twentieth century technology. We refuse to admit that today's fundamental changes must be changes in mind and spirit, not new technologies of offense or defense. Probably we blind ourselves to the dangers of modern warfare because very few of us have the courage to face the fact that survival is impossible in a war waged to the full with nuclear, chemical and biological weapons of unbelievable destructive power.

What kind of hope is possible? The recent, grievously disappointing decision of the Nixon Administration to go forward with an anti-ballistic missile system is a perfect example of this blindness, comparable to the blindness of the Johnson Administration in its pursuit of the Vietnam war.

Finally, we are still blind to the nature of power. David and Joan Baez-Harris pointed this out to us a few nights ago here at our church. We are still primarily motivated—even as governments were in the time of Jesus—by the love of power rather than the power of love. This love of power is very much a part of the Leningrad story and its aftermath, but it is also a predominant part of our United States of America story. Our national budget, with some 60% of it being directed toward military spending, is crystal clear evidence on this point. We are motivated more by the love of power than by the power of love. A denial of this fact is at best innocence, and worst, stupidity or hypocrisy.

What kind of hope is possible?

I think that none of us should answer this question lightly. Still, I know that I have to have hope in order to go on living, and I presume this is a universal need. The only viable hope is that which springs from a full acceptance of the dangers that face us, from compassion, and from a commitment to change our society.[12]

Memory is important. On the walls of the Piskarevsky Cemetery where the hundreds of thousands of victims of the Leningrad siege were buried in mass graves, the words of Olga Berggolts have been etched beside the eternal flame.[13]

Here lie the people of Leningrad,
Here are the citizens—men, women and children
And beside them the soldiers of the Red Army
Who gave their lives
Defending you, Leningrad,
Cradle of Revolution.
We cannot number the noble
Ones who lie beneath the eternal granite,
But of those honored by this stone
Let no one forget, let nothing be forgotten.

Let us remember these lines, and the lines of Anna Akhmatova, mourning the death of Valya Smirnov, a little Leningrad boy who was killed by a German bomb:

"Knock on my door with your little fist and I'll open it...
I did not hear you moan.
Bring me a little maple twig
Or simply a handful of grass,
And bring a handful of cold, pure Neva water
And I'll wash away the traces of blood
From your little golden head ..... "[14]

And let us remember the story of the boy who had compassion for a mouse:

"The thought of eating the mouse was repulsive. Finally he took the lid from the box, shook it and let the mouse escape. After all, he thought, the mouse was as hungry as he, and how did he know whether it did not have as much right to live as he did."[15]

*****

NOTES

1. Rabindranath Tagore, *Gitanjali, Song Offerings*, International Pocket Library, Macmillan, Paperback.

2. Harrison E. Salisbury, *The 900 Days, The Siege of Leningrad*, Harper and Row, 1969.

3. *Idem*, p. 477.

4. *Idem*, pp. 476, 477.

5. C.P. Snow, New York *Times Book Review*, Jan. 26, 1969.

6. *The 900 Days*, Chapter 46, Death, Death, Death, pp. 515 f.f

7. New York *Times Book Review*, above.

8. Luke 19:41-44.

9. We cannot comprehend the sheer destructive power of our own weapons. At one point we dropped more explosives on the perimeter of the Khe Sanh than "fell on Japan throughout World War II, and much more than fell on the whole of Europe during the years 1942 and 1943." (*New Yorker* Magazine, March 22, 1969, p. 30).

10. Again, statistics beggar the imagination. We are all comforted by talk of illusory defense measures. "I think all of you know there is no adequate defense against massive nuclear attack. It is both easier and cheaper to circumvent any known nuclear defense system than to provide it. It's all pretty crazy. At the very moment we are talking of deploying ABM's we are also building the MIRV, the weapon to circumvent ABM's.

"As far as I know the most conservative estimates of the number of Americans who would be killed in a major nuclear attack, with everything working as well as can be hoped and all foreseeable precautions taken, run to about fifty million. We have become callous to gruesome statistics, and this seems at first to be only another gruesome statistic. You think, Bang! and next morning, if you're still there, you read in the newspapers that fifty million people were killed.

"But that isn't the way it happens."

(George Wald, Professor of Biology at Harvard, and Nobel Prize Winner, *New Yorker* Magazine listed above.).

11. *The 900 Days*, p. 331 "Hitler insisted that von Leeb draw the tightest kind of circle around Leningrad. The Fuhrer instructed von Leeb that the city's capitulation was not to be accepted. The population was to die with the doomed city."

12. There are increasing numbers of men and women with the kind of hope which springs from recognition of cataclysmic dangers confronting us, a sense of compassion, and commitment to action. George Wald is one of them. He makes profound sense.

"About two million years ago, man appeared. He became the dominant species on the earth. All other living things, animal and plant, live by his sufferance. He is the custodian of life on earth, and in the solar system. It's a big responsibility.

"The thought that we're in competition with Russians or with Chinese is all a mistake and trivial. We are one species, with a world to win. There's life all over this universe, but the only life in the solar system is on earth, and in the whole universe we are the only men.

"Our business is with life, not death. Our challenge is to give what account we can of what becomes of life in the solar system, this corner of the universe which is our home; and, most of all, what becomes of men—all men, of all nations, colors and creeds. It is only such a world that can offer us life, and the chance to go on." (*New Yorker* Magazine listed above).

13. *The 900 Days*, pp. 582, 583.

14. *Idem* p. 364.

15. *Idem* pp 476, 477.

SELFHOOD

SELF-DISCOVERY

As far as I can isolate the meaning of "self"—as I think of the persons who are closest to me—the members of my own family, my colleagues in the ministry, the persons I work with, friends, the words that keep coming to mind are originality, uniqueness and individuality. We experience one another in so many different ways. There is sensory experience, physical appearance, touch, the sound of the voice, smell, and something also which is hard to describe—the word "presence" is about as well as I can do. "Presence" has to do with the wholeness of the impression which another person creates, but this wholeness may be caught up in the tiniest gesture, or even the tiniest hint of a gesture.

I had an experience here at the church a few years ago which will serve as an example. After the service, when I was greeting people as they left the church, a woman came up to me and said, "Harry, you know who I am." It was a crowded and pressured situation. "Yes," I said, with much more confidence than I actually had, "I'm sure I do." The woman was not going to let me off the hook. She planted herself firmly in front of me, and she said warmly, and with great firmness, "I'm not going to leave until you remember my name." There were at least three separate things that got through to me when she spoke. One was the timbre of her voice. Another was the brightness of her eyes. And the third was the sort of perky, up-beat tilt of her head and shoulders. It was the last that did it. Something like thirty-five years dropped away. The recognition came back with growing certainty. "You wouldn't be Jennie Nutter? You taught me French and Latin in high school."

We had a glad reunion. Suddenly she came back into my life after an absence of more than three decades. Her spontaneity, her courage, her great optimism, and her unfailing concern for her students—these qualities all were real again. It had been a long time since I had even thought of her, but when I saw her that day, with a rush of pleasure and gratitude, I realized how real a part of me she was.

We cannot understand ourselves until we grasp with our feelings the knowledge that we grow out of relationships which run far back to the forgotten periods of our lives. These relationships, though they have gone, so to speak underground, continue to remain potentially alive to the touch of memory and meeting.

Harry Overstreet tells of standing in a room looking at a rock collection. The collection was not distinguished by any special brilliance. His host switched on a particular kind of lamp, and suddenly the rock collection which had been prosaic enough until that moment leaped into life with color and brilliance. There are moments, and we all know them, when we meet a person or remember a person and the experience is one of illumination—or it may be of deep anxiety—introducing us to ourselves, restoring to life parts of ourselves that had become dormant or even dead.

the experience is one of illumination—or it may be of deep anxiety

I am saying several things here. One is that if we try to run away from our personal histories, it is because we are still shackled to them. The well-known rocket expert, Werner von Braun, testified a few days ago in connection with a Nazi War Crimes Trial. He said something that caught my attention. He said, "I had nothing to hide and I am not implicated. *I think everybody has to live with his past, however.*" I put these words over against the remark of Henry Ford, "It's all the same to me if a man comes from Sing Sing or Harvard. We have a man, not his history."

I think that both Ford and von Braun are right though they may seem to be saying things opposite to one another. We are not judged by our history but are judged by the way in which we relate to our history. It is a contemporary problem that minority groups in our country, which are given very few alternatives to crime, are often stigmatized for their criminal records by a society which virtually condemned them to criminality in the first place. But even these individuals have to come to terms with their own history in order to come to terms with themselves. Each of us has a personal history and that history is alive. If we cut ourselves off from it, we cut off part of ourselves. If we refuse to know it, we are truncated.

Each of us has a personal history and that history is alive

A man for whom I have great respect in these matters is Erik Erikson, Professor of Human Development at Harvard University. In his study of Martin Luther's life he describes the self as that which holds us together amidst all kinds of changes and experiences. The self is the constant in the midst of change. He uses the phrase, "sense of identity." He couples it with what it means to be adult. He writes:

> "To be adult means among other things to see one's life in continuous perspective, both in retrospect and in prospect. By accepting some definition of who he is, usually on the basis of a function in an economy, a place in the sequence of generations, a status in the structure of society, the adult is able selectively to reconstruct his past in such a way, that step for step it seems to have been planned for him, or better he seems to have planned it."[1]

To understand ourselves we need to have some feelings both good and bad—about how we became ourselves. There is rich nourishment for persons of all ages in good memories, strong memories of the past. And I refer not only to memories limited to one life-span; it helps to have good memories that span the generations. Alex Haley illustrates this in, *The Autobiography of Malcolm X*, and in his current work on his own black heritage.²

Erik Erikson is an authority, one of the greatest, on the ways in which young people seek to find themselves and to understand themselves. Again in his study of the young man, Martin Luther, he speaks of young people today who have temporarily lost, or who have never had *meaningful confirmation of the approved way of their fathers*. This comment of his is worth careful pondering:³

> The mocking grandiosity of their gang names (Black Barons, Junior Bishops, Navahoes, Saints), their insignia sometimes even tattoos in the skin, and their defiant behavior clearly indicate and attempt to emulate that which gives other people the background of a group identity: a real family, nobility, a proud history and religion.

We do not understand ourselves unless we understand our need for group identification, our need "to belong," our need to grow against continuous perspectives. These understandings are necessary if we are to feel sure of who we are, and not to be blown over, *uprooted* by every wind that blows. We find ourselves partly in positive feelings for our relationship to the past.

I am not advocating ancestor worship or tribal forms of belonging. I am saying, however, that the cultivation of personal uniqueness, the development of self-trust—all these things depend in part upon satisfactory relationships to the past, and the development of loyalties that go far beyond self-centeredness. Self-discovery takes place against a background of meaningful relationships, relationships good, bad and indifferent that we have somehow managed to put into a significant framework, and self-discovery teaches us that the past isn't as "dead" as we often think. It may come alive at the touch of a memory.

I don't want to seem to neglect the *now* aspect of self-discovery. If we are alive we are always discovering new and different potentialities in ourselves, even if in the end it be deepening potentialities in ourselves, even if in the end it be deepening resources of courage, trust and imagination with which to face "the end." Self-discovery brings the realization that what we think are "ends" often turn out to be "beginnings."

I had an unforgettable experience some fifteen years ago. We had invited the great Zen Buddhist scholar, Daisetz T. Suzuki[4] to lecture at our Unitarian Church in downtown Philadelphia. Incidentally when I first invited him to come, he turned us down because of the press of work. Then I wrote him again and asked him to recommend someone who, like himself, was a Zen Buddhist, knowledgeable in Zen Buddhist ways, schooled and knowledgeable in western thought categories, and able to interpret the East to the West and vice versa. I then received a rather plaintive note from him saying that since he was the only one he knew who met those qualification he supposed that he would have to come himself, and he did! I thought our correspondence was evidence of his acceptance of his own selfhood. There was no quality of vain and empty self-depreciation here!

I had the privilege of having breakfast with him the morning after his lecture. It was a tremendous experience for me to breakfast with one of the great religious figures of our time, a man who in my estimation ranked with Albert Schweitzer and Martin Buber. I must have been nervous as I sat across the table from this venerable patriarch. I did not mean to sound abstruse or to try to assume academic airs when *who do you think Jesus was?* I put my first question to him, but perhaps it did look as though I was trying too hard. I said, "Dr. Suzuki, how do you conceive of the Messianic role of Jesus?" He made no immediate answer and this rattled me further. I rephrased my question and said, "What I mean to say is who do you think Jesus was?" There was still no immediate answer. Instead, the Zen Buddhist sage regarded me quietly and then said in gentle fashion, "The important thing is not who I think Jesus was, but who you think you are. Who do you think you are?"

I was self-consciously defensive at this point and replied, "I could say that I am the sum total of all the relationships that I have ever entered into, the sum total of all the meetings I have had with all the persons in my life."

Again, there came a gentle rejoinder, "Yes, you could say that, but I think you would be verbalizing."

There was a longer pause on my part this time before I said, "I guess that I have to say that I don't know who I am."

And Dr. Suzuki said, "That's a very good place to begin."

I think it is a good place to begin, but not a good place to "end." In fact, I am inclined to think that living is made up of continuous beginnings. We begin over and over again and at the "end" of each beginning we find ourselves in "a new ball game," another now. Erik Erikson writes[5] that "healthy children will not fear life if their parents have integrity enough not to fear death." This is what I am saying. As we discover ourselves, our whole selves, we learn that while the past is always potentially alive in the present, the present is where we are. If we are not living there, where are we living?

The past is alive. The future is alive and the present is the place where they both meet. The present is where we uncover and discover our *being* and *becoming* potentials and where, as Abraham Maslow puts it, "time disappears and hopes are fulfilled."[6] It may also be the place where "beginnings" and "endings" disappear amidst the basic satisfactions of self-discovery, self-actualization, and self-fulfillment.[7] We can know the past without being imprisoned in it. We can face the future without being mesmerized by it—and we can live in the present.

The wonder of self-discovery can occur continually

The wonder of self-discovery can occur continually, not just yesterday, and not just tomorrow. It is the discovery of our own creativeness, or our own originality, of our unrealized growth potentials. It has been compared to many things: like getting the deed to your own house, like finding the golden slipper and knowing it fits your foot, like savoring the bitter-sweet taste of the pit of a peach.[8]

Richard Hughes in his, *A High Wind in Jamaica* gives us a beautiful description of a ten-year old child's moments of self-discovery:

> "And then an event did occur to Emily of considerable importance. She suddenly realized who she was. There is little reason that one can see why it should not have happened to her five years earlier, or even five years later; and none why it should have come that particular afternoon. She had been playing house in a nook right in the bows behind the windlass (on which she had hung a devil's claw as a door knocker); and tiring of it was walking rather aimlessly aft, thinking vaguely about some bees and a fairy queen, when it suddenly flashed into her mind that she was she. She stopped dead, and began looking over all of her person which came within the range of her eyes. She could not see much, except a foreshortened view of the front of her frock, and her hands when she lifted them for inspection: but it was enough for her to form a rough idea of the little body she suddenly realized to be hers.
>
> "She began to laugh rather mockingly. 'Well,' she thought in effect: 'fancy you, of all people, going and getting caught like this! You can't get out of it now, not for a very long time: you'll have to go through with being a child, and growing up, and getting old before you'll be quit of this mad prank.'"

I recently ran across material on the background of this lovely description of a child recognizing herself. A reader asked Richard Hughes if the incident was not, in fact, biographical. Hughes answered him:[9]

> "You have, of course, guessed right: the whole incident is based on the memory of my own childhood... I was around six or seven years. Oddly enough, when I was writing the book, I recollected it as happening to *me* just as casually as to Emily: but today I can't help wondering whether it wasn't triggered

by another incident I now recall separately: the almost unbearable spectacle of a cat playing with a live mouse. For sympathetically I identified with the hopeless tortured mouse: and it could be the discovery that I wasn't the mouse after all led on to the question, 'Well, in that case, who am I?' And so to the discovery that I was 'me.'"

That this experience of self-discovery came out of a child's early experience with a suffering mouse shows how closely related self-discovery is to the discovery of persons, animals, "things," the world "outside" the self.[10] It must have something to do with that characteristic of love described by Erich Fromm—"In love two persons become one and remain two."

*****

NOTES

1. Erik Erikson, *Young Man Luther*, W.W. Norton and Company, Inc., 1958, pp. 111, 112.

2. Alex Haley, Co-author with Malcolm X of *The Autobiography of Malcolm X.*, Grove Press, Inc., 1964.

Alex Haley is currently working on a new book which will trace his ancestry back to the point of its African origin. To listen to him talk about this book is to know the power and aliveness of the past! The working title of the book is: *Before This Anger*.

James Baldwin's words are also relevant: "But if a man understands his identity, his cultural background, then that man is no longer a slave." (Quoted in the San Francisco *Chronicle*, April 11, 1969)

3. Erik Erikson, *Young Man Luther*, pp. 114, 115.

4. I recommend two books for those wishing to know D.T. Suzuki, *Zen Buddhism, Selected Writings of D.T. Suzuki*, published by Doubleday Anchor Books, 1956; edited by William Barrett. *Zen Buddhism and Psychoanalysis* by Erich Fromm, D.T. Suzuki and Richard De Martino, published by Harper and Brothers, 1960.

5. Erik Erikson, *Childhood and Society*, W.W. Norton and Company, Inc., 1950, p. 233.

6. Abraham Maslow, *Toward A Psychology of Being*, Published by A. Van Nostrand Company, Inc., 1962, p. 200.

The passage deserves fuller quoting: "From Freud we learned that the past exists now in the person. Now we must learn from growth theory and self-actualization theory that the future also now exists in the person in the form of ideals, hopes, duties, tasks, plans, goals, unrealized potentials, mission, fate, destiny, etc. One for whom no future exists is reduced to the concrete, to hopelessness, to emptiness.... Of course, being in a state of Being needs no future, because it is already there. Then Becoming ceases for the moment and its promissory notes are cashed in the form of ultimate rewards, i.e., the peak experiences, in which time disappears and hopes are fulfilled."

7. The "basic satisfactions of self-discovery" does not mean "success," the end of "trouble," unmitigated bliss. Here again Maslow (*Psychology of Being*, p 196) describes our condition. "Self-actualization does not mean a transcendence of all human problems. Conflict, anxiety, frustration, sadness, hurt, and guilt can all be found in healthy human beings...... To be untroubled when one should be troubled can be a sign of sickness. Sometimes smug people have to be scared 'into their wits'."

8. Rollo May uses there illustrations which are taken from a poignant statement of one of his patients who describes her self-discovery, or, perhaps I should say "self-recovery." In this connection I like Maslow's statement on the pain of growth. Growth is not all fun and games. (*Psychology of Being*. p 190) "Growth has not only rewards and pleasures but also many intrinsic pains and always will have. Each step forward is a step into the unfamiliar and is possibly dangerous. It also means giving up something familiar and good and satisfying. it frequently means a parting and a separation, even a kind of death prior to rebirth, with consequent nostalgia, fear, loneliness and mourning."

9. From an article published in *Manas*, October 2, 1968.

10. From Erich Fromm's *Art of Loving*.

I think here, in this same connection, of a statement made in an unsigned article in *Manas* (Col XX No. 52, Dec. 27, 1967) "So, in the final analysis, the way a man thinks about the world and the way he thinks about himself cannot be really separated. By thinking about himself as inextricably related to the world, its problems, his problems, a man begins to find out what he truly is, or inwardly wants to be. The only insoluble problems are the problems which come from evading this discovery. It is perfectly natural that human beings in the mass should seem to present insuperable obstacles to the dreams of highly trained technical men who have all their lives studied a different order of reality, to the almost total neglect of man."

I cannot refrain from adding to Richard Hughes' mouse-experience the poignant story told by Harrison Salisbury in this account of the siege of Leningrad (*The 900 Days*, pp 476, 477).

"A mouse confronted one little Leningrad boy with a difficult moral problem. His grandmother had a tin box in which she put every extra scrap of bread and crackers. It was the family's 'iron reserves.' If all else failed—but only then—they would dig into the box. One day the boy was alone in the freezing flat. He heard an noise inside the tin box. He knew what this meant. A mouse was eating the iron reserves. He could not immediately decide what to do. Should he open the box and release the mouse? Should he open the box, kill the mouse and throw it away? Or should he kill the mouse and eat it? The last alternative was the one which most tempted him for, after all, the mouse had been consuming their food. But the thought of eating the mouse was repulsive. Finally, he took the lid from the box, shook it and let the mouse escape. After all, he thought, the mouse was as hungry as he, and how did he know whether it did not have as much right to live as he did?"

SELF-GROWTH

In Cora Mason's story of Socrates' boyhood[1] she describes a conversation which she fancies took place between Socrates and his father, the stonecutter, Sophroniscus. Sophroniscus is shaping a lion's head from a block of marble. Socrates asks him how he knows where the lion is. Sophroniscus replies that first you have to see in the lion in the stone, a prisoner there, waiting to be freed. Then you take your tools and begin the delicate work of removing the stone which imprisons him. That takes great skill and patience. But finally, after you have done your work, he stands clear, set free, and beautiful.

This is too simplistic a picture of self-finding, but there are elements of truth in it. The self has its own dynamism. It is not passively waiting to be found, it is engaged in self-creation. It grows through interaction. The better metaphor is organic or biological. It is like a plant and sunlight interacting. "No ray of sunlight is ever lost, but the green which it wakes into existence needs time to sprout." We grow from our centers. We have our own dynamic properties. We grow from our relationships with others.

A short time ago, I had a wonderful experience of growth with my eight months old grandson. He was sitting on my lap. I was trying to talk with him—not words, just sounds. He began to talk with me. I would make a sound. He would reply with a similar sound. I would raise my voice a bit, he would raise his. I would lower mine, and he would follow suit. We were face to face, and he regarded me with a degree of attention and complete absorption which it would be hard to surpass, and I reciprocated. Every facet of his posture spelled communication. We were not using words, but there was no doubt in my mind that we were present to each other. His mother and grandmother were in the room with us and they regarded this encounter as being as intense and meaningful as I am reporting it. It lasted perhaps three or four minutes, and then he decided it was time to eat. We were sitting at the kitchen table, and he made it plain that he wished to go to his high chair. I was left to speculate on the meaning of this remarkable "conversation." We had come close together in it. We had reached and met one another with sounds, and touch and hearing and seeing. We had grown together. The static metaphor of the lion in the stone would not describe it as accurately as the organic one of growth through reciprocity of influence.

growth potential is in us from the beginning

This growth potential is in us from the beginning. Carl Rogers calls it "the mainspring of life."[2] It is released and stimulated by other persons, by environment, by "outside" forces and influences. Unfortunately, we are not always open to the forces about us that can help us to grow. We do not always perceive how our openness is a potent factor in our grow-ability. We do not always understand how true it is that we can become ourselves only as we lose ourselves, i.e., give ourselves to something other than ourselves, so that without any diminishing of our independence and individuality—if anything, it becomes enhanced—we become the agents and instruments for larger purposes.

Alex Haley, "co-author" of *Malcolm X's Autobiography*, spoke here in San Francisco a few months ago. He described how events which we think are in our hands and our control may gradually take us over. He was talking about his forthcoming book—its working title is *Before This Anger*, in which he traces his ancestry back more than two centuries to the African village from which his ancestor was abducted, to the very slave ship which brought that ancestor to

Annapolis, Maryland in 1767. Listening to Haley speak is a most satisfying experience. He is such a gifted and sensitive man and such a superb story teller. But apart from the substantive merit of his forthcoming book, which is very considerable, I was struck by his description of what happened to him *personally* in his remarkable quest to discover his history as a black man. He is talking about a journey into self-hood. There came a point, he said, when he felt that he was no longer alone in his pursuit of his ancestors. He felt as though he was being accompanied in the quest by the people he sought—that as he walked over the hills of the part of West Africa where they had lived, they came to meet him. He was no longer digging out facts in a unilateral effort, the facts were now seeking him out. He had become part of events larger than himself. He was not so much writing as being written.

Certainly, many of us have had the feelings which he described so powerfully. Sometimes when I am working on a sermon, I seem to be standing in the way of what I want to say because I am trying too hard to say it. I am pushing, pushing, pushing, striving, striving, striving! Here is a sentence. There is a sentence. Here is an idea, and over there is another one that can somehow be joined to it. Sometimes when I am at the point of desperation in my frustrations, I go away, give it up, "sleep on it" and when I come back, I no longer stand in my own way. I feel that the ideas and thoughts I struggled to find are now finding me. I am not expressing myself, I am being expressed. I am not speaking so much as being spoken through. I experience a paradox here. At times I grow by struggling and striving. At other times I grow by getting out of my own way, by being quiet, and waiting and listening. In this latter state, events, purposes, the day itself speaks to me. My part is to keep channels clear, that is, not to let myself become so cluttered up that I can't hear what is being said.

> *I grow by getting out of my own way*

I am sure that this is one of the things Martin Buber means when he says that all real life is meeting.[3]

We grow as we learn to hear that part of ourselves which comes through "on its own." I experience this as part of myself and as more than part of myself. It is described in so many different ways. I find the following description significant:

> "Buried in the deepest stratum of the unconscious, at the wellspring of man's existence, lies an immense psychological force. In pure form, it is experienced as a longing, the object of which is constantly receding from him, as the horizons of his world widen throughout his growth. It begins, perhaps with the infant's amazing discovery that the breast which brings it comfort is not part of itself, but actually belongs to another sentient being. From that moment longing drives the human organism to relate himself to, to comprehend, in the deepest sense to "love" that which lies beyond him. Any experience of this longing, either in oneself or others, is cause for delight. This is because it brings with it its own insight and therefore the seeds of its own fulfillment."[4]

This longing finds its fulfillment in many ways and in many experiences. It is satisfied when we experience a sense of oneness with the natural world, a sense of participation in the earth's trustworthiness or beauty. Such moments may bring a quiet kind of self-renewal—-or they may bring what Emerson called "perfect exhilaration."[5] It feeds on experiences of wonder. It is nourished in moments of glad recognition by others—recognition of our worth as persons. It is nourished by warm and affirming personal relationships, and by *achievements*, particularly in the area of self-expression. Sometimes it appears to be extremely fragile, as though it could be easily crushed. But some psychologists like Abraham Maslow[6] are coming to see it as biologically rooted, i.e. grounded in the nature of things. Its fragileness then is the fragileness of all life. If it is rooted in the nature of things as we understand them, this does not mean that it is indestructible. With the advent of nuclear, chemical and biological means of destruction, we have had to revise our estimates of what can be destroyed and what cannot be destroyed. It appears that we can destroy life on this planet, if we will.

But assuming the continuation of our life on the planet, then this longing is a durable force. Even in the midst of inhuman systems of our own devising, its voice can be heard. Heavy as the odds may be against it, it can "get through" if there are any openings whatever. It is a kind of original health, a primary force, and it is a most important part of the experience we have of ourselves. As to whether or not it gets expressed by us, and through us, and how, it appears that nothing is much more important than the setting of priorities and the factor of deliberate choice. Our choices are made both consciously and unconsciously. It is the latter, the unconscious choices, which are implied in the commonly used phrase, *depth of character*. So much of what we call character lies below the surface.

> *this longing is a durable force. Even in the midst of inhuman systems of our own devising*

It is my experience that when I make value-choices consistently, consciously, deliberately, over a period of time—and not always without pain and difficulty—they work themselves into my nature below conscious awareness and become part of my hidden self. Then these choices may become a kind of tune or melody which seems to play itself. After a while, I do not have to deliberately choose to hear it. It comes unbidden as though I had given it the key to my house. It comes when it will, of its own volition.

This is one reason why the deliberate setting of value-priorities is so crucial to self-growth. We *can* choose the directions in which we wish to grow. If we do not deliberately choose, "choices" are made by default. Eventually, as I have indicated, the choices we make, deliberately, consistently, over a period of time, seem to choose us. It is sometimes a question in my mind whether we own what we own or whether what we think we own actually owns us. And it is sometimes a question, too, whether we choose or are chosen by the purposes—trivial or important—which are dominant in our living.

I remember a woman in my childhood who, during the long summer days, was always chasing house flies. No matter who was in the house, no matter what absorbing conversation was going on, if there was a fly in the house, she was up and after it. I know there were good reasons for this excessive concern for a fly-free house. But it must have been a burden, because if there was a fly in the air, she couldn't see anything else: neither the sun, nor the trees, nor the flowers, nor the earth, nor the people, nor whatever of beauty or importance there was in that day. Because she was a bright woman and very much alive, she could chase flies and seemingly miss very little of what was going on around her. But it always seemed to me that the focus on flies must have limited and impaired her ability to be open to other realities. It always seemed to me that flies had taken possession of her!

I am aware from personal experience, as well as from the observation of others, that it is easy to let ourselves be dominated by preoccupations which choose us simply because we do not exercise our freedom of choice in any significant fashion. We permit ourselves to be taken over by trivialities, or worse than trivialities, by destructive, impoverishing forces, purposes, ideologies which actually choose us because we have made no choices ourselves. They choose us because we are "empty." We may be neat and tidy, but the significant thing is that we are empty.[7]

My experience tells me that the chief ground for optimism with respect to our future is the remarkable capacity we have to change ourselves. I am continually impressed by the ability of individuals to open doors and windows on new vistas of selfhood and by the ability we have at all ages and in all conditions to discover and rediscover in ourselves new and larger sources of health and strength. The usual problem in changing ourselves and in self-finding is not a lack of growth potential. The problem is that we have not made the choices, developed the loyalties, established the priorities, made the decisions which will bring those potentials into being. I am struck both by the positive and negative implications of these words of Abraham Maslow:

> "Capacities clamor to be used and cease their clamor only when they *are* well used. That is, capacities are also needs. Not only is it fun to use our capacities, but it is also necessary for growth. The unused skill or capacity can become a disease center or else atrophy or disappear, thus diminishing the person."[3]

How constantly we diminish ourselves by not using the capacities which are already part of us. Selfhood, personhood is not something that happens by the grace of God, or by the accident of being born into a particular family in a particular age. Families both help and hinder growth to selfhood. We cannot deny the influence of environment. The point I stress, however, is that we can be our own worst enemies in this area as in others. Self is both achievement and gift. It is in the interplay between the *given* and the *achieved* that we grow. We can change. We do change. We are changed, by circumstances, by others, *by ourselves*. We have immense learning capacities which can be focussed outward, enabling us to bring about desperately needed changes in our external environment. But these learning capacities can also be focused inward. Then they help us to free and to utilize those positive human capacities which *clamor to be used and which cease their clamor only when they are well used.*

Pogo is right, of course, when he says, "We shall meet the enemy. He shall be ours. He may be us. Forward!"

*****

NOTES

1. Cora Mason, *Socrates—The Man Who Dared to Ask*, Beacon Press, 1953 pp 12 ff.

2. Carl Rogers, *On Becoming a Person*, Houghton Mifflin Co. 1961 p. 35.

"Gradually my experience has forced me to conclude that the individual has within himself the capacity and tendency, latent if not evident, to move forward toward maturity.....Whether one call it a growth tendency, a drive toward self-actualization, or a forward-moving directional tendency, it is the mainspring of life, and is, in the last analysis, the tendency upon which all psychotherapy depends. It is the urge which is evident in all organic and human life—to expand, extend, become autonomous, develop, mature ...."

3. The phrase occurs in his *I and Thou*, (Charles Scribner's Sons, 1958 p. 11).

"The primary word, 'I-Thou,' can be spoken only with the whole being. Concentration and fusion into the whole being can never take place through my agency, not can it ever take place without me. I become through my relationship to the Thou; as I become I, I say Thou. 'All real living is meeting.'"

4. This description was written by a psychiatrist, Robert C. Murphy, Jr. in a Pendle Hill Pamphlet published in 1960 entitled, *Psychotherapy based on Human Longing*.

5. Emerson wrote, "Crossing a bare common, in snow puddles, at twilight, under a clouded sky, without having in my thoughts any occurrence of special good fortune, I have enjoyed a perfect exhilaration, I am glad to the point of fear."

Quoted in *The Practical Cogitator*. Edited by Charles P. Curtis, Jr. and Ferris Greenslet. Houghton Mifflin Company 1945. p. 117.

6. I have in mind Abraham Maslow's conclusion found in his, so far as I know, unpublished paper, *A Theory of Metamotivation: The Biological Rooting of the Value Life*. p. 19.

"The spiritual or value-life then falls well within the realm of nature, rather than being a different and opposed realm. It is susceptible to investigation at once by psychologists and social scientists, and in theory, will eventually become also a problem for neurology, endocrinology, genetics and biochemistry as these sciences develop suitable methods."

7. I associate here to a New Testament passage, Luke 11:24 ff.

"When an unclean spirit comes out of a man it wanders over the deserts seeking a resting place; and finding none, it says, 'I will go back to the home I left.' So it returns and finds the house swept clean and tidy. Off it goes and collects seven other spirits more wicked than itself, and they all come in and settle down; and in the end the man's plight is worse than before!" This state could be called "clean and tidy emptiness." I have been thinking of it as the state of no commitments, no choices, and this is certainly "emptiness."

8. From Abraham Maslow's *Toward a Psychology of Being*, D. Van Nostrand and Company, Inc. 1962, p. 187.

OUR UNCONSCIOUS SELVES

Sometimes people talk about the unconscious as though it were Sigmund Freud's private invention. No one would have been more amused at this kind of talk than Freud himself. Freud's *dream book*[1] appeared in 1900. This was a most significant part of his theories of the unconscious. It is such a beautifully written book that reading it is an esthetic experience. It has been called Freud's most original work[2] and it is particularly fascinating because it is one of the fruits of his own self-analysis. One reads it and understands why Freud considered dreams to be the royal road to the unconscious.

Dreams themselves have long been understood as bearers of significant messages. Erich Fromm prefaces his book, *The Forgotten Language*,[3] with two quotations about dreams—one, of pre-Christian origin, from the Talmud, and the other from Emerson's essay on *Demonology* written some 17 years before *The Interpretation of Dreams*.

From the Talmud: "A dream which is not understood is like a letter which is not opened."

From Emerson: "Sleep takes off the costume of circumstance, arms us with terrible freedom, so that every will rushes to a deed. A skillful man reads his dreams for his self-knowledge; yet not the details but the quality."

We cannot understand ourselves if all the images we employ to describe ourselves are devoid of the dimension of depth. I think that in our age, which is the age of the machines. we tend to think of ourselves too rationalistically. We tend to put an excessive value on predictability and to limit the range of the spontaneous and the unpredictable in our thought and conduct. We try to understand ourselves too much in terms of what is see-able, what can be filed and catalogued, what is on-the-surface. We tend to underestimate the importance of such forgotten languages as dreams, and myths and fairy tales. Freud did not invent the unconscious. He discovered, uncovered or recovered it, and we need to do likewise.

It as all a bit like the oil underneath the Santa Barbara Channel which being "let loose" has created so much havoc along the coast of southern California. Because I do not have the training of a geologist, I find it hard to know how scientists and technologists knew there was oil there to begin with, and I wonder that they had sufficient faith in their hypotheses and technical know-how to go below and try to get it out. There are some parallels that could be drawn here, had we the time, between the danger of releasing the forces of the unconscious and the danger of letting subterranean oil deposits loose without the proper understanding. But I am interested primarily in the fact that the oil was there, beneath the land which was beneath the ocean, which was beneath the drilling platform, which was beneath the feet of the drillers who stood beneath the sky. There was much more to the scene than met the eye prior to the coming of the geologists and their technicians.

Freud perceived through self-analysis as well as in his treatment of his patients that dreams are a mysterious language. He used them to track out mental pathologies. He described them as royal roads to the unconscious part of ourselves. There were some other highways to the unconscious. He knew that, and charted some of them, too. But he felt that dreams were the straightest and the quickest of all highways.

I know this to be true, because my own dreams afford a degree of self-insight which is very helpful. I have the same feelings about them that Emerson had about his dreams. My interest in dreams was stimulated and developed during a 10-year pastorate at the First Unitarian Church of Philadelphia when I became interested in psychoanalysis. I undertook an educative analysis and in 1957 I graduated from the Philadelphia Psychoanalytic Institute. This does not qualify me as a practitioner of psychoanalysis, but it does give me an extensive psychoanalytic background against which to practice the ministry. As part of the educative program, I underwent a psychoanalysis. I want to say a couple of things about it.

I was brought up short last year by a comment which the psychoanalyst, Erik Erickson, made to Richard Evans.[4] Evans asked Erikson about the relative value of psychoanalysis when compared to less intensive methods of treatment. Erikson responded that psychoanalysis may not be the best method of therapy in all cases and then said, speculatively, that it may be "applicable to much more than therapy...It may be the principal form of systematic introspection and meditation." He goes on then, in substantiation of the point to recall the book, *Zen Buddhism and Psychoanalysis*, written by three men, Eric Fromm, Daisetz D. Suzuki and Richard D. Martino[5]

> *psychoanalysis may be the principal form of systematic introspection and meditation*

What happened to me when I read Erikson's comment relating psychoanalysis to meditation was a flash of my recognition. I, too, had made that discovery in my own time and in my own way. I had discovered that the hundreds of hours I spent on an analytic couch accounted for much of the flavor and form of the meditative patterns which I have developed over the past ten to twelve years. The analytic interview in its classic form is an exercise in disciplined freedom. You are bound primarily to one rule: to say what you think and feel without holding anything back; to let the process of free association have full play. I think of Kenneth Patton's words.[6] "A man is many wires strung in the wind, and he must sing the song of the air that flows over him."

On the analytic couch you say what flows over you, or what flows out of you. You give up for a time the process of conscious selectivity which characterizes our habitual ways of speaking and relating, and you let that other part of yourself, the unconscious, take over. In this process you become aware of the oil under the channel, you become aware of the extent to which you necessarily exercise control upon your ways of expressing words and feelings in your normal day-to-day experiences and relationships. You become aware of the customs and inhibitions which prevent us from disclosing the whole of ourselves. You become aware of the paradox that you are what you seem to be, and that you are not what you seem to be: You become vividly aware that there is a lot more to us than which appears *on the surface*—which, by the way, is a revealing, common phrase—*appears on the surface.*

there is a lot more to us than which appears

It was a nice experience for me to have a brilliant psychoanalyst like Erickson link meditation and psychoanalysis together. And it is, I think profoundly insightful of Erich Fromm to attempt to bring Zen Buddhism and psychoanalysis together, seeking sources of common wisdom, but not ignoring their differences either.

I have learned that one way to overcome the common disassociation of consciousness and unconsciousness and to recapture a sense of wholeness it to practice the kind of listening to self which lets the whole of the self come through. I do this in different ways, sometimes over a period of time—weeks or months and even years—at a regular hour. Sometimes on a non-scheduled basis, picking opportunities as they come. Sometimes I walk or sit doing nothing except waiting for the whole of me to gather to make way for feelings and thoughts which may have been driven virtually out of sight and hearing by external pressures. Often, after a period of waiting, I put forward a poem or a fragment of writing which has special meaning for me and let it draw thoughts and feelings around it. It is like a magnet, or "bait" for fishes below the water's surface, and feelings surround it. It speaks to the part of me which has gone underground, and that part of me is brought back to consciousness. I find words like these words of Kaye Dunham[7] a stimulus to whole self-recovery:

> *Let wonder replace fear*
> *Life is the God-dream*
> *Let wonder replace fear*
> *Then will come the*
> *Deep significance of being.*

Of course the coming of the "deep significance of being" means that the fears must come forth, too, and the hates, and impulses to destruction and self-destruction. The get-thee-behind-me-Satan parts of ourselves need to be met. They also need to know that they are not beyond hospitality. It has always interested me that in the prologue to the Book of Job when God held open house for his sons, his son, Satan, was not excluded. "Now there was a day when the sons of God came to present themselves before the Lord, and Satan came also among them."[8] The problem with cutting off recognition of the Satan-part of ourselves is that in holding back the Satan-part we may unwittingly hold back the God-part also. What does it mean in the Book of Job that Satan is also one of God's sons? I would think it means that there is no clear line of demarcation between "good" and "bad", creative and destructive, life and death, etc. I would think it meant that to be whole, we have to learn to listen to and to accept the whole of ourselves.[9]

One of the ways I try to know the whole of myself is by seeking to understand what my dreams say to me. For some 15 years, I have written down dreams which I consider of particular interest. I'll offer two by way of example, one without comment and one with some interpretation.

Dream One—*without interpretation*:

I am seated on a platform with a man who is chairing a meeting. He is seated beside me. I have put a speech manuscript on the narrow pulpit. The man introduces me, saying, "We are so happy to have him with us, and we want him to speak freely as though in the open air."

I get up and look at my manuscript, which is actually a series of sketchy notes, and realize that I am expected to speak freely, spontaneously, without even notes, relying on memory, and the inspiration of the moment.

The mood of the dream is friendly. I feel easy and confident.

Dream Two—*with some interpretation*:

I am present at a meeting of our church Board of Trustees. In the midst of the meeting one of the Board members insults me gratuitously. I feel hurt and wounded. But what astonishes me is that immediately after this the rest of the Board falls into a most raucous quarrel, pushing and shoving one another to the point where I think physical violence is going to break out.

My feeling in this dream was one of hurt and concern, but not of terror or panic. I am anxious, but feel that the Board will survive these difficulties.

I can assure you that what happened in the dream is not what happens at our Board meetings—at least not *on the surface*. What had happened *in reality* as we say—as though the dream was not also a *piece of reality*—what had happened took place at a Board meeting held the very night of the dream. There was a discussion at the Board meeting of raffles as a method of fund raising. I made it plain that I did not think much of raffles as a way of financing our church program. One of the members of the Board took the opposite point of view. Another member said, with a smile, "You're making Harry unhappy." The first member replied, "I don't think it is the function of this Board to make the Minister happy." It was a fairly normal exchange, taking place in an atmosphere which was basically open and frank, but not unfriendly. I doubt that I would have thought anymore about the discussion of my unconscious had not picked it up that night, and worked it over at the level of some fairly primary anxieties.

What, then, was my unconscious up to? And how did it perform its mission? It began by making it clear that the church boards of trustees are the natural enemies of ministers. Beyond and below that it hitched onto certain fears I have of the undependable, precarious nature of authority figures and institutions—fears which go back to my early childhood, and are readily understandable in the light of the character of that childhood. It gave my anxieties a sharp and bizarre twist, by pointing out that my Board of Trustees in particular is not to be trusted. It said in effect, "They will insult you, if they get a chance, and they are also out to destroy your happiness. You heard what they said to you tonight—that they do not exist to make you happy. You know what that means? That means that they do exist to make you UNHAPPY!" It continued, "They are supposed to be examples for everyone in the church to follow, dependable, reliable, considerate, but they insult you and then fight among themselves until they are likely to bring that handsome new building down around their heads and yours."

fears I have of the undependable, precarious nature of authority figures and institutions

In the morning's waking light the dream was disappearing fast as though it did not want to be caught out in broad daylight. But I wouldn't let it go. I have developed some persistence in these matters. When I am trying to capture a dream I remind myself of a robin standing on our front lawn, legs braced, beak attached to a worm, striving valiantly to pull the worm out of the ground while the worm strives just as valiantly to get back to the underworld which is his proper home. I pulled that dream out into the morning light, and enjoyed the interesting picture it has painted, a picture not to be ignored, but not to be taken literally either. I enjoyed its capacity to exaggerate. I enjoyed its capacity to give full expression to feeling without regard to any fine discriminations. It reminded me that there is a part of me that over-reacts to the slightest hint of criticism. It told me that I have the capacity to take reasonable disagreement and treat it as though it were total rejection. It told me that I have the capacity to feel rejected when I am in fact warmly accepted. It reminded me that when I became a man, St. Paul to the contrary notwithstanding—I did not "put away childish things." Few of us ever do completely.

And that is alright, for while childishness may be inappropriate in the adult, childlikeness is of great and enduring value. I was glad, via the dream, to talk with one of my selves and to hear what he had to say. I was glad to accept him as one of my large family of selves. And I am glad to introduce him publicly.

The words "conscious" and "unconscious" are not easy words to understand. And even as I use them, I am afraid of presenting too sharp a distinction between them as though they were at opposite ends of the pole, which they are not. The point I am most concerned to make is that to accept the whole of ourselves we have to learn to know what lies below the surfaces, to respect it, to listen to it—even to nourish and to cherish it. We have to understand the value and the meaning of its "forgotten language." We have to learn to value and to heed spontaneous impulses as well as the value of disciplined thought, a bit of wildness as well as lots of order, the messages of myths, dreams, fairy tales and phantasies as well as the language of reason, art as well as logic.

Putting it briefly—we will do well to heed the wisdom of the Talmud: "A dream that is not understood is like a letter which is not opened."

Also we will do well to heed Emerson's observation: "Sleep takes off the costume of circumstance, so that every will rushes to a deed. A skillful man reads his dreams for his self-knowledge; yet not the details, but the quality."

*****

NOTES

1. The *Dream Book* was actually published in November of 1899, but the publisher chose to put the year 1900 on the title page. Six hundred copies of the book were printed. It took 8 years to sell them. (See Vol. 1 p. 360, *The Life and Work of Sigmund Freud* by Ernest Jones, Basic Books, Inc., 1953).

2. Ernest Jones considers it Freud's major work, his most original work and "the one by which his name will probably be longest remembered." (Vol. 1 p. 350, *The Life and Work of Sigmund Freud*)

3. Erich Fromm, *The Forgotten Language*, Grove Press, Inc, 1951, pp 140 ff.

Erich Fromm describes Emerson's statement in these words, "One of the most beautiful and concise statements on the superior rational character of our mental processes in sleep." He quotes in at length. It is from Emerson's essay on *Demonology* published in 1883.

4. Richard I. Evans, *Dialogue with Erik Erikson*, Harper and Row, 1967, pp. 95-96.

5. Erich Fromm, D.T. Suzuki, Richard D. Martino, *Zen Buddhism and Psychoanalysis*, Harper and Brothers, 1960.

6. Kenneth Patton, *Readings for the Celebration of Life*, Meeting House Press, 1957, p. 18.

7. Kaye Dunham, *I Tell You, I Tell You, I Tell You*, Privately circulated.

8. Job, 1:6.

9. Martin Buber has helped me in this area as in many others. I think of two passages in his writings cited by Maurice S. Friedman in his Martin Buber, *The Life of Dialogue*, Harper and Brothers, 1955, p. 102.

The first is a quotation from Buber's *Images of Good and Evil*.

"A man only knows factually what "evil" is in so far as he knows about himself, everything else to which he gives this name is merely mirrored illusion ... self-perception and self-relationship are the peculiarly human, the irruption of a strange element into nature, the inner lot of a man."

The second passage is from Buber's *Between Man and Man*. Beacon Press, 1955, pp. 78, 79. "Good and evil, then, cannot be a pair of opposites like right and left or above and beneath. 'Good' is the movement in the direction of home; 'evil' is the aimless whirl of human potentialities without which nothing can be achieved and by which, if they take no direction but remain trapped in themselves, everything goes awry. If the two were indeed poles, the man who did not see them as such would be blind; but the man would be blinder who did not perceive the lightning flash from pole to pole, the 'and.'"

SELF-ACTUALIZATION IN TOUGH CIRCUMSTANCES

It is often helpful to me when I am facing personal problems to think of myself as living in two worlds. This two-world concept, which is so much a part of contemporary psychology, has long roots in scriptural writings. In the Old Testament, in the Book of Micah, we find the familiar words, "What does the Lord require of you but to do justly, love mercy and walk humbly with your God."[1] I think of this injunction as pointing to the importance of commitment and action in the external world, the world "outside" us. In the New Testament—"The Kingdom of God is within you."[2] These words, of course, point to the "inner world."

Our inner world is described by psychologists in the formidable phrase, "intrapsychic organization."[3] It is a subjective world, but none the less real for that. It is a world of feelings, hopes, fears and wishes. It is the place of that uniqueness, that idiosyncratic style of being and doing which is me. It is a world of dreams and phantasies, of buried but not "dead" memories. It is a world of potentially potent remembrances and of forgotten languages. I discover this from time to time—discover and rediscover—that there are forces in this inner world of mine which make for wholeness and strength and health. They take various forms and speak in various languages. There is a host of good impulses within me which I constantly ignore or, at best, give a passing glance of self-recognition. They encourage me toward greater openness, trust, love, self-acceptance, a more positive appreciation of others, a higher expectation of life, a wiser understanding of suffering. Theirs is often a gently voice which goes virtually unheard amidst the loud noises which come pounding in from the "outside" world. For reasons which all of us could readily list, we get out of touch with this inner spirit. It is our sadness at being out of touch with ourselves at the deepest level which gives Stephen Spender's familiar lines their poignancy and relevance.

> *What is precious is never to forget*
> *The essential delight of the blood drawn from ageless springs*
> *Breaking through rocks in worlds before our earth.*
> *Never to deny its pleasure in the morning simple light*
> *Nor its grave evening demand for love.*
> *Never to allow gradually the traffic to smother*
> *With noise and fog, the flowering of the spirit.*[4]

"The flowering of the spirit" has a great deal to do, as I see it, with wise self-acceptance and with the acceptance of others. A number of psychologists today seem to me to be working this terrain even when their terminology is dissimilar. I think of Carl Rogers and some of the "learnings" he writes of in his autobiographic essay, *This is Me.*[5] "In my relationships with persons I have found that it does not help, in the long run, to act as though I were something I am not" ... "I find I am more effective when I can listen acceptantly to myself, and can be myself..." "I have found it of enormous value when I can permit myself to understand another person" ... "The more I am open to the realities in me and in the other person, the less do I find myself wishing to rush in to 'fix things'." It seems to me that Rogers is speaking of a kind of growth-process which gets beyond sterile, egocentric individualism. Somehow, the I becomes the manifestation of more than the I, and a flowering of the self takes place which cannot be kept within the bounds of any self-centered egotism.

I can listen acceptantly to myself

It represents a staying-in-touch-with-yourself way of living which is sensitive to the many currents which flow within and around us.

I think that initially, at least, it takes real effort for us to stay in touch with ourselves. Several years ago the actors group known as "The Committee" here in San Francisco put on a simulated therapeutic interview in which the therapist was a computer. The skit made a tremendous impression on me. I have never been able to forget it. The client sits in a room with a computer and they engage in a dialogue together. The computer is so awesomely smart! It knows a great deal more about the patient than the patient knows about himself.

Remembering this skit, I have sometimes wondered how it would go with me if I had a little computer which was designed to keep me in touch with myself. He is a gentle though authoritative fellow and I fancy such dialogue as this: (Note how already I am personalizing him.)

> Computer: "Harry, I'm afraid you are getting out of touch with yourself again. You are trying to shape your thoughts and actions too much by listening to others. Why don't you try listening to yourself?'
>
> Harry: "What do you mean? I'm not sure I understand you."
>
> Computer: "You say you live in two worlds. I heard you say it publicly in church. The only world you seem to be conscious of is the world *out there*. You've forgotten that you have a center."
>
> Harry: "I'm trying to stay in touch with myself. I really am. As a matter of fact, I agree completely with Carl Rogers when he says ...."
>
> Computer: "You don't have to validate yourself by appealing to Carl Rogers. You are like a tape recorder, repeating what other people say. Why don't you quote your own experience? Why don't you move from your own center? Harry! What is

happening to your center! It looks like a basement completely filled up with other people's furniture!"

I'm not sure what would happen if I had this computer on my shoulder—probably one of three things. I might start climbing the walls. I might throw the marvelous computer off the Golden Gate Bridge. I might just start experiencing myself more fully.

I experience an *inner* world, and I experience an *outer* world. The second part of this operational picture, the outer world, is the world of external events, pressures, realities. As the inner world has the two dimensions of the *given* and the *made*, the *discovered* and the *created*, so does the external world. There are areas and events for which I take primary responsibility. There are other areas which may be described as fate, "happenings," Providence—you name it. The important fact is that I am not responsible for many of the things which overtake me. I did not create them. I had nothing to do with their falling into the orbit of my existence. I just have to live with them.

the inner world has the two dimensions of the given and the made

This is a most familiar theme in literature. Hamlet discovers—note the word *discovers*—that the major burden of his life is determined for him by an event which was in no sense of his own making, his uncle's murder of his father and marriage to his mother. When this dawns on him, he cries out,

> *The time is out of joint; O cursed spite,*
> *That ever I was born to set it right.*

Let me try to put this human dilemma in contemporary terms, putting it in the first person though obviously the "I" is not always appropriate.

"I did not ask to be born black in a white, racist society."

"It was not my wish or my doing to be stricken with terminal illness at the age of 26."

"I had nothing to do with my mother's suicide at the age of 5. How can I be expected to accept that?"

"I did not choose to be born on the eve of the First World War, to graduate from high school on the eve of the Great Depression, to come out of graduate school as the country entered World War II."

"I did not choose to be born a Jew in Hitler's Germany. I escaped by the most far-fetched chance. The rest of my family was incinerated."

"I had nothing to do with causing the drunken rages of my father. Why should I be stuck with them and my memories of them?"

These two worlds in which we live, the one of external events and the other of psychic realities—they are not in separate orbits, though they are quite different. They criss-cross and intersect one another. Sometimes they seem to be on a collision course. It seems at times as though the external world tries to rub out the inner world. My inner life sometimes seems like a candle flame threatened by a high wind. My inner world itself may be the scene of storms that come from within rather than from the outside.

How do you bring your two worlds together? How do I bring *mine* together? I begin by recognizing that these worlds are not alien to one another. By processes we are only beginning to understand, they feed us and support one another. Even the hard things that happen to us—the profound interior splits and struggle—the "outside" inevitables may themselves embody deepening experiences. It is no masochistic glorification of adversity to see that the untoward happenings, tragedies which we thought at that time they overtook us would crush utterly, became open roads over which we travelled to deeper self-realization and service.

This does not happen without pain, for while growth may for the most part be pleasurable there are times when it is virtually synonymous with pain.⁷ The bleak, irrational, terrible, incomprehensible experiences with ourselves had through ourselves with others. It doesn't always happen. But it happens more often than we realize. One of my favorite descriptions of it happening is in the lines of Emily Dickinson:

A death-blow is a life-blow to some
Who 'till they died, did not alive become;
Who, had they lived, had died, but when
*They died, vitality begun.*⁸

Health and wholeness means putting our hands to tasks in the outer world which we cannot complete but which we are never entirely free to neglect. Again and again when we commit ourselves to action moving into the outer world to achieve a personal reconciliation to face hate and misunderstanding with good will; to act for peace; to act for justice; to break the fetters we thought unbreakable⁹ to do the thing that previously we have been afraid to do; to risk ourselves for truth, as we understand it, then the very act of moving into the outer world pulls our inner world together. When we seek to remake the outer world, we begin to reshape ourselves. We release energies within ourselves that have too long lain dormant.

Ibsen writes of one of his characters: "Edith was a little country bounded on the north, south, east and west by Edith."

When we hug ourselves too tightly, we diminish ourselves. When we cut ourselves off from others, we deny ourselves resources of health and wisdom. When we stand in our own way, everything stands in our way.¹⁰ When we are too exclusively oriented to the outer world or too excessively wrapped up in the inner world, the power of perception is blurred.¹¹ Our inner and outer worlds draw nourishment from one another. In deep relationships and in the fulfillment of significant purposes we lose ourselves to find ourselves.

It is only as the two worlds in which we live rub against, collide with and interpenetrate each other that we are able to feel at home in them, to go back and forth between them, to be renewed in their meeting with one another.

It is true that often the "tough circumstances" which we think threaten our existence from the outside are shadows we cast over ourselves from the inside. How may times we have worried and agonized over dangers and fears which did not materialize, which were, in fact, creations of our own minds. Whenever we do this we know from experience what Kierkegaard meant when he wrote that how to be *rightly* anxious is the main thing. But it is also true that circumstances can be as existentially hard, as dire, desperate and tragic as we had thought them to be even in our bleakest moments. We find, then,—I think all of us have seen this happen—that being at home in two worlds is of immense help. We may find that we can accept these *hopeless* circumstances with a quality of grace and courage that was not possible for us until we began to know ourselves, to act from ourselves, to trust ourselves, to be ourselves, and to share ourselves.

> *how to be rightly anxious is the main thing*

The psychiatrist, Kenneth Appel, tells of the following incident which has meanings that extend far beyond the physician-patient relationship. I think is says a lot about interpenetrating worlds:[12]

> "There was a psychotic patient who was desperately ill, lonesome, lost and bitter. She had been deserted by her spouse and children. Sedatives, except in sleep-producing dosages, gave no relief. Despite agitation some communication was possible. She was in a panic. The only recourse was medication for sleep.... I went to my office, obtained a copy of Thornton Wilder's *The Woman of Andros* and read for one half-hour to her about the heroine Chrysis' reflections on life as she approaches death: Chrysis raised herself on one elbow and her hands opened and closed upon the cloths that covered her ...

as she said, 'I want to say to someone ... that I have known the worst that the world can do to me and that nevertheless I praise the world and all living. All that is, is well. Remember some day, remember me as one who loved all things and accepted from the gods all things, the bright and the dark. And do you likewise. Farewell.'"

"In these words were healing. They brought meaning, atonement and forgiveness to my patient. Her healing did not come from understanding the dynamics of her condition but from a shared experience of high aesthetic quality that enabled her to rise about personal sorrow, to accept the pain of universal suffering, assimilate it without bitterness and move on to other areas of normal living and health."

*****

NOTES

1. Micah 6:8.

2. Luke 17:21.

3. Abraham Maslow described the "inner" and the "outer" worlds and their relationship to one another with a special kind of realism and clarity.

"It seems clear now that confusing these inner and outer realities, or having either closed off from experience, is highly pathological. The healthy person is able to integrate them both into his life and therefore has to give up neither, being able to go back and forth voluntarily. The difference is the same as one between the person who can visit the slums and the one who is forced to live there always. (Either world is a slum if one can't leave it) Then paradoxically, that which was sick and pathological and the "lowest" becomes part of the healthiest and "highest" aspect of human nature. Slipping into "craziness" is frightening only for those not fully convinced of their sanity. Education must help the person to live in both worlds." (*Towards a Psychology of Being*, D. Van Nostrand Co. Inc., 1962, p. 198).

4. It may be that we are becoming a bit less self-conscious about using the word "spirit." I like Huston Smith's words: "... man's spirit—defined as that level of the self where faculties distinguishable at more conscious levels as intellect, will, and emotion interpenetrate and act in concert—faces the unending task of perceiving meaning in ever-widening areas of human experience. (Huston Smith, *Condemned to Meaning,* Harper and Row, 1965, p. 46).

5. Carl Rogers, *On Becoming A Person*, Houghton Mifflin Company, 1961, pp. 15 ff.

6. Erik Erikson, *Insight and Responsibility, Lectures on the Ethical Implications of Psychoanalytic Insight*, W.W. Norton and Company, Inc., 1964, p. 149.

7. Again, Maslow is very relevant: "Growth has not only rewards and pleasures but also many intrinsic pains and always will have ... It frequently means a parting and a separation even a kind of death prior to rebirth, with consequent nostalgia, fear, loneliness and mourning." (*Toward a Psychology of Being*, p. 190).

8. *The Poems of Emily Dickinson*, Little Brown and Company, 1930, pp. 177.

9. Even the non-believer can appreciate the substance of A. Powell Davies prayer, "Teach us, O God, that when our fetters seem too strong to break, the time has come at last when we must break them." (*The Language of The Heart*, Farrar, Straus and Cudahy, 1956 by A. Powell Davies. p. 52.

10. In October of 1842, Emerson wrote in his journal, "Henry Thoreau made, last night, the fine remark that, so long as a man stands in his own way, everything seems to be in his way, governments, society, and even the sun and moon and starts, as astrology

may testify. (*The Heart of Emerson's Journals*, edited by Bliss Perry. Houghton Mifflin Company, 1928, p. 189).

11. William Blake's observation comes to mind: "If the doors of perception were cleansed, everything would appear to man as it is, infinite. For man has closed himself up, 'till he sees all things through the narrow chinks of his cavern." (*Thoughts for Meditation*, arranged by N. Gangulee, Beacon Press, 1952, p. 33).

12. *Making the Ministry Relevant*, Edited by Hans Hofmann. Charles Scribner and Sons, 1960, pp. 91, 92.

THE FAITH OF SIGMUND FREUD

The only way to describe a man's real religion is to describe his life. I would do this with respect to Sigmund Freud. I would, however, make some preliminary observations. Freud himself would probably have objected to the word "religion." He has no use for religion as such, although he respected the manner in which certain clergymen utilized the findings of psychoanalysis in their religious vocation. Instead of religion, he would have suggested, perhaps with irony, some such phrase as "world outlook," "personal philosophy," or the German term *weltanschauung*, which he did use as the title of an important lecture.

I am using the term "religion" in a nonconventional sense. I do not use it as signifying belief in the existence of a personal, supernatural deity. Far from believing in the existence of God, I think Freud would have agreed with the unbeliever who said that a theologian looking for God was like a blind man looking in a dark cellar for a black cat which was not there! By religious belief, I mean belief in the paramount worthwhileness of certain ethical values which have grown out of human life, which are essential to human survival, and which are at the core of ethical monotheism as they are also at the core of scientific humanism.

If we define religion in terms of acceptance of traditional theological beliefs, then Freud does not come within the circle. If we define religion not as submission to a Higher Power, which is the standard definition, but rather as commitment to ethical values, then Sigmund Freud was a man of great faith, even though he was called—and I think rightly, from the conventional point of view—an unrepentant atheist.

Let us look then at Freud's life and, more obliquely, at his works, to ask ourselves what they tell us about his personal faith. The life was a long one and of such epoch-making significance that he deserves to be ranked with Einstein, Darwin and Newton. To treat it as briefly as I treat it is to treat it crudely indeed.

The biographical outline of the life is simple enough. He was born of Jewish extraction at Freiberg in Moravia on May 6, 1856. He died in London on September 23, 1939. When he was four years old, his family moved to Vienna, and there he lived practically the whole of his life. He was the founder of psychoanalysis.

He believed preeminently in the power of the human intellect and he relied on his own mind with confidence and stoutness. He relied on his mind with a consistency and thoroughness which few men have achieved. Darwin's *Origin of Species* was published in 1859. Writing late in life, Freud looked back at himself as a teenager, and what he recalls tells us something of his early predisposition to intellectual interests. He writes that as a youngster, he was strongly attracted to the theories of Darwin because he was convinced that they held out hopes of an extraordinary advance in man's understanding of the world. It was when he was perhaps seventeen, and was much interested in Darwin, that he heard a professor read aloud Goethe's essay on Nature. Under the stimulus of this beautiful essay, he decided that he would go into the practice of medicine.

His biographers differ on what the essay actually meant to him. One, Wittels, says that it was not only the sense of unity and beauty which Goethe found in nature and which he set forth so eloquently in this essay that attracted the young boy, but it was also the questions of meaning and purpose which the essay raised. Ernest Jones, the man who may have known him best, perhaps better than the members of his own family, disagrees. He says that it's doubtful that Freud "ever cudgeled his brains about the meaning of the universe." Whether Jones is speaking of Jones or Freud is a moot point. It would seem to me that a man who was as much concerned with religion as Freud—Freud wrote more on the subject of religion than on any other subject except psychoanalysis itself—and who was as much concerned with the existence or nonexistence of God, however unrepentant an atheist he might be, must nevertheless have been deeply concerned with the riddle of the universe.

It was characteristic of Freud and a mark, I would say, of his personal religion, that he knew how to be an agnostic. He knew how to live with life's great uncertainties. He conceived it to be his mission not so much to establish immutable truths as to raise questions. Part of his faith was his belief in the importance and the power of questions. He believed that nothing was more important than that man should search for truth, but for him no truth was divinely revealed. There was only the truth to be discovered by intellect. He was, so far as I know, completely indifferent to every kind of mysticism.

> **He knew how to live with life's great uncertainties**

Genius has been defined, I think, by Alfred North Whitehead, as the capacity to analyze the obvious. Freud met the test supremely. Did men make slips of the tongue? Did they commit little errors that were meaningless? Why did they think the errors were meaningless? Why? Why? Why? Out of this "why" came his book: *The Psycho-pathology of Everyday Life*.

Why was the religion of the believer similar in some respects to the patient suffering from obsessional neurosis? What were the beginnings of religion? How could one correlate the religion of primitive man with the religion of civilized man? Why? Out of this "why" came one of the three books that he considered his most important: *Totem and Taboo*."

Sex, what was it? What was the relationship between neurosis and sexuality? Could it be that children had a sexual life, and why? Why was sex so hush-hush that not even doctors dared to talk about it? They talked only to one another, and that very quietly. Why? And out of this "why" came the second book which he considered among his three most important: *Three Contributions to the Theory of Sex*."

And dreams; everybody had them and ignored them. What was the cause of last night's dream—the hot mince pie, the lobster, the strawberries with that rich sour cream? What is a dream and why does a dream so curiously distort reality? And out of those "whys" there came what he considered his third major opus, the great and beautiful *Dream Book*. "What a silly thing," said many of his colleagues, "for a grown-up scientist to write about dreams!" But now we know that dreams were, as he himself said, a royal road leading to the unconscious.

dreams were a royal road leading to the unconscious

He believed, and this is implicit in his works and in his life, in the liberating, healing power of truth.

It has been said that the entire burden of the religion of the New Testament is revealed in the story of the disciples of Jesus walking through a cornfield on the Sabbath Day. Jesus is criticized because the hungry disciples break off the ears of corn and eat. He replies to his critics with a saying which is certainly central to understanding the essence of his religion, "The Sabbath was made for man, and not man for the Sabbath."

We turn to the life and the work of Freud and we say to ourselves, What a simple thing the analytic situation is. "The aim of the analytic cure," writes Erich Fromm, "is to replace the irrational, the Id, by reason, the Ego. The analytic situation may be defined from this standpoint as one where two people, the doctor and the patient, devote themselves to the search for truth. The aim of the cure is restoring health, and the remedies to sickness are truth and reason. To have postulated a situation based upon radical honesty in a culture in which such frankness is rare is perhaps the greatest expression of Freud's genius."

As in the cornfield incident, so in the analytic situation we see a man's values. There is belief in compassion, and there is compassion for suffering manifest to an extraordinary degree. There is a devotion to truth in a new setting, which makes us apply in a fresh way the familiar verse of the Gospel of John: "Ye shall know the truth and the truth shall make you free." Free from what? Free from the irrational compulsions of an unconscious which has never been explored. There is a deepening application, because the unconscious is now recognized, of the driving force of the great Socratic injunction, so important in the history of Western civilization, the injunction: "Know thyself." There is, and how significant this is in an age of conformity, a respect for the individual, which says, in effect: My relationship to one person, if it be at a deep enough level, is more significant by far than my relationship to a multitude. To be truly known, men must be known as individuals and not en masse. And there is implicit in this analytic situation at its best, the sign and token of a pioneering venture which makes meaningful the words of Francis Quarles: "Why dost thou wonder, O Man, at the height of the stars or the depth of the sea? Enter into thine own soul, and wonder there."

> *To be truly known, men must be known as individuals and not en masse*

Devotion to truth, compassion, freedom from the irrational, self-knowledge, individualism, respect for reason, a pioneering spirit: these are the values implicit in the analytic situation itself, that unique device for the exploration of the mind, which was conceived by Freud. How are these same values implicit in the life?

Freud believed that the traditional religious answers to death and suffering were pathetically absurd. They were strong, he granted, but they were strong because they corresponded with what is infantile and wishful in the human psyche. He believed that death must be accepted as that which is ordained by fate and to which there is no answer save the answer forged by human fortitude and courage, the answer revealed in renewed devotion to the tasks of living. His faith, a faith in man rather than a faith in God, did not falter when he had to meet the death challenge within his own family.

the answer revealed in renewed devotion to the tasks of living

The Freuds had six children. As I write this, I recall an experience I had on a plane traveling across the country. I was reading Jones' work on Freud, and the man who was sitting opposite me—I suspected him of being a clergyman—leaned over and saw what I was reading. He said, "It must have been difficult for a family to live with a man who had wicked ideas such as he had." Well, the family didn't seem to be too much troubled by his "wicked ideas," and the family life was perhaps more happy and full than most family life is.

One of the six children was a beautiful daughter named Sophie, who was a source of much delight to the parents. They called her their "Sunday" child. On a day in January, 1920, came the news of her sudden death. She was only twenty-six and had been in perfect health and happiness. She died of pneumonia. She left behind her two children, one of whom was only thirteen months old. The news was a thunderbolt. It came on the evening of the day that Freud had lost one of his closest associates, who died suddenly at the age of thirty-nine. Wrote Freud to his friend, the clergyman Oscar Pfister, "She was blown away as though she had never been." And then to one of his more intimate colleagues, he tried to describe his reactions: "I do not know what more there is to say. It is such a paralyzing event, which can stir no afterthoughts when one is not a believer and so is spared all the conflicts which go with that. Blunt necessity, mute submission."

Three years later, Sophie's child, then four and a half, had his tonsils removed at the same time that Freud underwent his first operation for what was to become an epic struggle with cancer. When the four-year-old boy and the sixty-seven-year-old man came together to talk over their operations, the boy said to his grandfather with great interest, "I can already eat crusts. Can you too?" Unfortunately, the boy was very delicate, "a bag of skin and bones," and he died shortly afterwards as a result of tuberculosis.

It was the only occasion in his life that Freud was known to shed tears. He told Ernest Jones afterwards that the loss of this child had affected him in a different way from any other loss he had ever suffered. He said it was as though this death had killed something in his personality for good, and he could never recover from the loss. Three years later, he told a friend who had lost his eldest child, that the little grandchild, Heinerle, had stood for him for all children and grandchildren. "Since the child's death," he said, "I have not been able to enjoy life." He added, "It is the secret of my indifference—people call it courage—toward the danger to my own life."

> *I prefer to think in torment rather than not to think clearly.*

Freud believed that the answer to suffering was to overcome it, if possible, by such means as might be evolved through science; but where such means were not successful, then suffering must be accepted. A man must work it through, so far as possible, by his devotion to people, by devotion to his chosen work, and by living out his values. This Freud did in the second struggle I wish to allude to, the struggle with cancer.

It was in 1923, when he lost his grandson, Heinerle, that he underwent his first operation for cancer of the mouth. There were to be thirty-three more operations before death released him from the long struggle. Until close to the end, even when in great pain, he was unwilling to use drugs. He said, "I prefer to think in torment rather than not to think clearly." Surely this remark tells us a good deal, both about his value system and the tenacity with which he held to the values in which he believed.

How a man faces a disease of this sort, cancer, which gradually ate its way through his palate until it was impossible for him to eat, tells us something about the deeper resources and the deeper religion by which he lived. Freud came to look upon the cancer as a worthy adversary. "There is no longer any doubt," he wrote to a close personal friend in the year of his death, 1939, "That I have a new recurrence of my dear old cancer with which I have been sharing my existence for sixteen years. Which of us would prove stronger at that time we could not predict." The "dear old cancer" proved stronger. Due to its ravages, he slipped away quietly and very willingly in his comfortable home in London on September 23, 1939. He had, as he admitted again and again, no hopes of another world, but in meeting the long period of suffering which always had the face of death behind it, he rose above it as far as it is given to most of us to rise above these things.

He bore the pain stoically. He was remarkably free from irritability. He was patient with his doctors. He was deeply concerned with the needs of others—with the members of his family, with his patients, and with the affairs of his own colleagues. On occasion, he was even wryly humorous. So on the day that World War II broke out, which was the month of his death, a radio commentator said, with that omniscience which radio commentators sometimes indulge, that one thing was sure: this was the last war. Freud was asked what he thought of this prediction, and he answered dryly, "Anyhow, it's my last war."

"Anyhow, it's my last war."

The last book he read was one of Balzac's stories, dealing with hunger. He was at this time unable to eat. He commented that this was a very appropriate book for him to read because its focus was on starvation.

There are many remarkable stories in the annals of human history about men and women meeting illness. Robert Louis Stevenson is a great example of one who lived creatively, although he lived his life in the most fragile health. Franklin Delano Roosevelt was another who rose far above the illness which sometimes crushes others. And Freud, struggling with cancer: if we look at the chronology of his productivity we would never guess it. In 1923, the first operation; in 1927, *The Future of an Illusion*; in 1929, *Civilization and its Discontents*; in 1932, the *New Introductory Lectures*; and in 1938, the year before he died, *Moses and Monotheism*."

Freud believed that where suffering had to be met, it should be faced without fantasies. He had no theological solution to the problem. Once he was asked what the main things were to learn in life; and whether the questioner expected a complicated answer or not, he got a very simple one. Freud answered him, "*Zu arbeiten und zu lieben*," to labor and to love. It seems to me that this was the answer Freud gave to sickness, to suffering and to death. In the face of these, he sought to labor and to love.

If we look at Freud's life, not through his theories, which often seem so pessimistic, but through his responses to the afflictions which confronted him, I think we see that there are elements in it which were more than stoical, which indeed sound a note of triumph. There are two instances which I would cite on this point. The first has to do with his professional career; the second with his exile.

In the course of formulating his theory on the causes of hysteria, he discovered in 1914 that he had not made a far-reaching blunder in assuming that the stories of childhood seduction, related to him by his patients, were true facts and not fantasies. There came a point then where the theory seemed in danger of breaking down because he had misinterpreted the data on which it was based. For a time, he confesses, he was thrown into the deepest bewilderment. At last came the reflection that a man has not the right to despair because he has been deceived in his expectations; he must simply go ahead and revise them. So he recognized his blunder and he did it in a singular way which I think portrays a kind of bedrock optimism. He wrote to his intimate friend, Wilhelm Fliess. He confessed the error and he confessed something that was extremely curious; he confessed that though he ought to feel ashamed of having made the error, he did not. And then he paraphrased a beautiful text from the Book of Samuel: "Tell it not in Gath, publish it not in the streets of Askelon, in the land of the Philistines, but between you and me, I have the feeling of a victory rather than of a defeat."

Freud's great hero, and this is paradoxical for a man who had so little use for traditional religion, was Moses. The Biblical passage from which this text—"Tell it not in Gath, publish it not in Askelon, lest the daughters of the Philistines rejoice"—is taken from the Ode of Lamentation written by David over the death of Jonathan and Saul. Freud was like David, a slayer of Goliaths. He was like the ancient patriarchs of Israel, ready to set forth on journeys the end of which he could not see. Yet, journeying ever in a wilderness, he was convinced of the worthwhileness of the enterprise. He seemed to feel in his bones that he was making a long journey toward truth. I say he traveled the road by faith, faith in those universal values which lend dignity and beauty to human life.

Freud was proud of his Jewishness, even though he was not a monotheist. "I gladly and proudly acknowledge my Jewishness though my attitude toward any religion, including ours, is essentially negative....We Jews have always known how to respect spiritual values. We preserved our unity through ideas, and because of them we have survived to this day." Eventually, because of his Jewishness and his ideas, he felt the whip of anti-Semitic brutality and stupidity. In May, 1933, the Nazis did him the signal honor of burning his books in Berlin. In June, 1938, his friends and colleagues finally persuaded him to leave the Nazi-dominated Vienna.

Now look at him to see the nature of his personal faith. Here he is, an old man, 82 years, with a bad heart, with cancer which, within a short time would become inoperable, with his books burned, with Europe close to the throes of war—here he is, facing a barbaric recrudescence of anti-Semitism and fleeing one of the worst dictators that history has ever known. And what happens?

During the night journey from Paris to London, he had a dream. What does a man dream when he flees the Nazis? Freud dreamed that he was landing at Pevensey. He told the dream to his son, but his son did not understand its significance. The old man had to explain to him that Pevensey was the town on the English coast where William the Conqueror had landed in 1066! Indeed, this does not sound like a depressed and beaten refugee fleeing the lash of tyranny in fear and trembling; nor does it sound like a man whose religion, at its core, was simply the acceptance of the inevitable. It brings to mind the great triumphant ones of history: Joseph, who saved the people of Israel from starvation and who also believed in his dreams; Moses the lawgiver, Freud's great hero; David, the slayer of giants, the builder of Jerusalem; William the Conqueror.

Here is a triumphant man who, however he breaks with the tenets of ecclesiastical orthodoxy, believes greatly. He believes in the power of truth, in the strength of the mind, in the healing nature of intelligent compassion, and in the dignity of each human person. Even as he traverses the boundaries of the human psyche, looking into its depths as few men have ever done, he has the courage to believe in himself.

GROWING TOWARD PERSONHOOD

GROWING TOWARD PERSONHOOD I

DEEP DECISION MAKING

This past year I have had the opportunity to read some of the works of one of the greatest American psychologist—some would call him the founder of American psychology—William James. I have long been impressed with the fact that the so-called "third force" psychologists[1] who are a very broad group, including many psychologists who pitch their tents between dogmatic Freudianism and dogmatic Behaviorism, are sympathetic to the religious. They are sympathetic to William James pragmatic, inquiring open-minded attitude toward the religious.

This past summer, out of my interest in these "third force" people, I undertook an unusual project. I read together—I might almost say simultaneously—William James' *Varieties of Religious Experience*[2], and Abraham Maslow's *Toward a Psychology of Being*. I did this reading in an interesting and profitable fashion by literally interlacing the one with the other. First I would read a chapter of James' *Varieties* and then I would read a chapter from Maslow's *Towards a Psychology of Being*. Then I would let the two streams of thought mingle together, and seek to understand their interrelatedness. As I worked my way along, I mixed into these converging streams a later book of Maslow's entitled *Religious Values and Peak Experiences*[3] The opening sentence of that book describes its lineage.

"This lecture is in a direct line with James' *Varieties of Religious Experience,* John Dewey's *A Common Faith* and Fromm's *Psychoanalysis and Religion.* They examine religious experiences as psychologists examine any experience, descriptively, empirically, humanistically in an effort to be as truthful as possible."

examine any experience, descriptively, empirically, humanistically in an effort to be as truthful as possible

It struck me at the time that I could hardly have found a single sentence touching more directly on three books more influential in my own intellectual and spiritual evolution.

Subsequently, I had an opportunity to talk with Abraham Maslow about the way in which I had been commingling his and William James' thought. I can't quote him exactly, but he said something to the effect, "What you did was most appropriate for James was my great teacher." And he went on to describe what James had meant to him as a teacher, a man and a person.[4]

Of course, one of the things that makes William James such a powerful teacher through the written as through the spoken word, is his fullness of personhood. I suppose that is the ultimate aim or test of a great teacher—the fullness of his own being as a person. James' fullness as a person was extraordinary. I have always been particularly moved and influenced by the many ways in which his teachings on the nature of will and decision-making flowed out of his own life, his personal experiences with indecision, ill health—all his fears and anxieties around the meaningless of life—not life in the abstract, but his own particular life. He wrestled in desperation until his late twenties with agonizing doubts as to whether his life had any meaning—any meaning at all! Then there occurs in his journal a passage which is a lodestar with respect to the power and the nature of human will :[5]

"I think yesterday was a crisis in my life. I finished the first part of Renouvier's 2nd essay, and saw no reason why his definition of free will—'the sustaining of a thought *because I choose to* when I might have other thoughts'—need be the definition of an illusion. At any rate I will assume for the present—until next year—that it is no illusion.

"My first act of free will shall be to believe in free will. For the remainder of the year, I will abstain from the mere speculation and contemplative *Grublei* (musing, meditation, meandering thoughts) in which my nature takes most delight, and voluntarily cultivate the feeling of moral freedom, by reading books favorable to it as well as by acting. After the first of January, my callow skin being somewhat fledged, I may perhaps return to metaphysic study and skepticism without danger to my powers of action. For the present, then, remember: Care little for the speculation .... Much for the *form* of my action."

This is a passage from a man's journal. I consider it a great passage in the history of psychological literature, and in religious literature also, if religious literature be, as I think it is, the record of our inner struggles for a sense of direction, for meaning and wholeness. It is directly concerned with the ancient theological issues of man—freedom and meaning.

Someone has said that phrases like *free will*, *moral freedom* and *determinism*, *fate* no longer fire our imaginations. They don't in the abstract. I don't know that they ever did fire masses of people as abstract propositions, but when they are concrete they still reach us. James was concrete—concretely concerned with his strengths and *weaknesses*, *his* identity, *his* personal health, wholeness, goodness and badness.

a phrase of Plato's— "A whole man is a whole will"

He was struck by a phrase[6] of Plato's—"A whole man is a whole will." It meant to him that willing and choosing isn't just one little department in our personalities, marked ego. This will is not simply a cranial agent, an act of the mind. Will is a process which calls into mind every facet of ourselves: blood stream, heart beats, the nerve endings along the skin, sight and hearing, imagination, hope, fear—everything. A whole person is a person in whom more or less consistently, certainly at high moments, all the *willing* agents come together in one piece. When we choose, *really* choose, we choose with our whole selves, the intellect, the body, the emotions, the mind—the whole organism. Full choosing is an organismic response to existence. This is deep decision making.

I would like to drive home the point by underscoring the mood and range of issues which hit James very hard at his particular moment of deep decision. This was just about 100 years ago April 30, 1870. He was 27 years old and from that day he would be able to will at a more unified depth than he had ever achieved before.

At this same time that he was receiving help from the writings of the French philosopher, Charles Renouvier, who was touching him at the level of the realness of his own willing, and the reality of his own choices he was also receiving great practical help from the British psychologist, Alexander Bain, particularly from Bain's understanding and analysis of the importance of habit in making deep decisions stick.

Again there occurs in James' journal a passage addressed to his own difficulties in following through on what he willed to make happen.[7] He wrote these words to himself:

> "Recollect that only when habits of order are formed can we advance to really interesting fields of action—and consequently accumulate grain on grain of wilful choice like a very miser, never forgetting how one link dropped does an indefinite number."

But the passage in his journal that is pivotal—the April 30 passage—is as follows. My reference to Bain will make it clearer:[7]

"Today has furnished the exceptionally passionate initiative which Bain posits as needful for the acquisition of habits ... in accumulated acts of thought lies salvation ... Hitherto when I have felt like taking a free initiative, like daring to act originally, without carefully waiting for contemplation of the external world to determine all for me, suicide seemed the most manly form for me to put my daring into; now I will go a step further with my will, not only act with it, but believe as well; believe in my own individuality and creative power. My belief to be sure can't be optimistic—but I will posit life (the real, the good) in the self-governing resistance of ego to the world, life shall be built in doing, in suffering and in creating."

James discovered for himself, and out of himself—the discovery could not be real for him until it came out of himself—that back of the will to act is the will to believe. "*...now I will go a step further with my own will, not only act with it, but believe as well; believe in my own individuality and creative power.*"

Are we born with knowledge of our own individuality and creative power? If we are, it would appear that many of us lose it, and have to rediscover it before we can truly claim it as our own. There is an element of conscious choice here. We opt for creative rather than destructive power. We opt for the kind of individuality which centers on separateness to the denial of being at one with all persons.

Another thing we are told here about decision making is that deep decisions do not come easily. We have a strange fantasy that we should be able to make painful decisions without pain! This may go back to the primeval paradise out of which we have fallen. But as William James' experience shows, deep decisions often come hard. James is in the school of the Apostle Paul at this point anyway, "The good that I would do, I do not, and the evil that I would not, that I do."

The kind of psychology and theology in which I am putting my faith these days, does not deny that we are—in ourselves—often divided, conflicted, torn up, torn asunder. Still it seeks to overcome and reconcile the disparate "selves" which make up any one self. It brings the varied selves together in acts of willing. But it does not presume that the "unity" achieved is an automatic "unity."

This belief that it is possible to reconcile the divisions within ourselves into a unified will and purpose seems to me to be itself a kind of faith-assumption, more perhaps religious than scientific in character. I feel that underneath it there lies an undeniable faith assumption which is clearly stated in the words of psychologists who work in what might be called the "third force" tradition[1] The assumption is that in their deepest essence human potentialities move toward goodness, that the deepest reality in our humanness is creativity, and that at the very heart of our natures is what has been called "emergent beauty."

Now I link up these assumptions of the "third force" psychologists with those teachings which are a long and powerfully beautiful part of the religious humanistic traditions.

I think of the saying attributed to Jesus of Nazareth—"The Kingdom of God is within you."[8]

We might think also of the so-called secret sayings of Jesus:

Lift the stone and you will find me;
Split the wood and there I am.[9]

But the affirmation is found again and again in humanistic strains in all religions and non-religions. There is a saying that comes to me through the writings of a young black poet, Kaye Dunham.

"Honor each moment for in it one is taking part in a miracle, the miracle of existence."

Contemporary psychologists say it more prosaically, but they say it. The words are Abraham Maslow's:[10]

"There is now emerging over the horizon a new conception of human sickness and of human health, a psychology that I find so thrilling and so full of wonderful possibilities that I yield to the temptation to present it publicly even before it is checked and confirmed, and before it can be called reliable scientific knowledge."

The basic assumptions of this point of view are:

1. We have, each of us, an essential biologically based inner nature, which is to some degree "natural," intrinsic, given, and, in a certain limited sense, unchangeable, or, at least, unchanging.

2. Each person's inner nature is in part unique to himself and in part species-wide.

3. It is possible to study this inner nature scientifically and to discover what it is like (not *invent—discover*).

4. This inner nature, as much as we know of it so far, seems not to be intrinsically evil, but rather either neutral or positively "good." What we call evil behavior appears most often to be a secondary reaction to frustration of this intrinsic nature.

5. Since this inner nature is good or neutral rather than bad, it is best to bring it out and to encourage it rather than to suppress it. If it is permitted to guide our life, we grow healthy, fruitful, and happy.

6. If this essential core of the person is denied or suppressed, he gets sick sometimes in obvious ways, sometimes in subtle ways, sometimes immediately, sometimes later.

7. This inner nature is not strong and overpowering and unmistakable like the instincts of animals. It is weak and delicate and subtle and easily overcome by habit, cultural pressure, and wrong attitudes toward it.

8. Even though weak, it rarely disappears in the normal person—perhaps not even in the sick person. Even though denied, it persists underground forever pressing for actualization.

9. Somehow, these conclusions must all be articulated with the necessity of discipline, deprivation, frustration, pain, and tragedy. To

the extent that these experiences reveal and foster and fulfill our inner nature, to that extent they are desirable experiences."

These are faith assumptions, as I see them, and powerfully important ones, which the wise learn to live.

I close with some words of Robert Frost which speak to the point:

"Earth's the right place for love.
I don't know where it's likely to go better."

And some kindred words of Walt Whitman's:

"I say that the whole earth and all the stars in the sky are
for religion's sake.
I say no man has ever yet been half devout enough,
None has ever adored or worshiped half enough,
None has begun to think how divine he himself is
and how certain the future is."

*****

NOTES

1. Abraham Maslow, *Toward a Psychology of Being*, D. Van Nostrand Co., Inc. See p. viii for a description of the "Third Force."

2. William James, *The Varieties of Religious Experience*, Longmans, Green and Company, 1902.

3. Abraham Maslow, *Religions, Values, and Peak Experiences*, Ohio State University Press, 1964, p. XI.

4. This was in a conversation with Maslow in the fall of 1969. In recent years few people have had as much influence on my thinking as has Maslow. He was a very great teacher even for those who knew him chiefly through his books. I am very deeply indebted to him.

5. Gay Wilson Allen, *William James*, The Viking Press, 1967, p. 168.

The passage was written by James on April 30, 1868.

6. Above, Gay Wilson reference, p. 164. "On January 5 (1870) after reading Plato, he copied, as if making it his motto: *"Ein ganzer Mensch-ein ganzer Willer"*—"A whole man is a whole will."

7. Gay Wilson Allen reference, p. 169.

8. Luke 17:21.

9. *The Secret Sayings of Jesus According to the Gospel of Thomas,* Fontana Books, 1960.

10. *Toward a Psychology of Being*, (Maslow) pp. 3,4.

11. *Secret Sayings of Jesus According to the Gospel of Thomas.*

GROWING TOWARD PERSONHOOD II

WILLING AND CHOOSING

An act of will or choice is related to prayer. This may surprise us because we are often inclined to think of prayer as an obsolete custom springing from crudely supernaturalistic religion; but consider this prayer of Socrates which Rollo May writes "might well be inscribed on the wall of every therapist's office,"[1]

> "Beloved Pan, and all ye other gods who haunt this place, give me beauty in the inward soul; and may the outward and the inward man be at one. May I reckon the wise to be the wealthy, and may I have such a quantity of gold as none but the temperate can carry."

I don't know how old Socrates was when he uttered that prayer. I believe he might have offered the prayer at any time. All his life he retained a sense of the wonder and freshness of life. He never lost his joy in life, his wonder at life, his sense of life as a gift.

We might say that this attitude—accepting life as a great and wondrous gift—is possible in relatively placid times but not in the frightening, difficult times in which we live. I suspect that such and observation would only betray our ignorance of history. Socrates, too, lived in a society which was threatened with destruction and was in a state of transition. In his old age he was on trial for his life with the verdict almost certain to run against him. He was on trial on trumped up charges that he had corrupted the youth of his city and denied the gods' existence. A few says ago, at his installation as president of the University of San Francisco, Rupert Johnson described Socrates as the first victim of the urban crisis. This certainly makes him our contemporary!

It is not far fetched for me to assume that this prayer could have been uttered—such was the undying spirit of the man—in the midst of that urban crisis and his personal crisis. Our essential character is reflected in our prayers. If we boggle at the word "prayer" then let us say in our deepest wishes and longings. And we have some say as to what those longings and wishes will be. They may well up finally from the unconscious part of our beings, but it is we who open particular doors, and we who cultivate particular currents in our own beings. José Ortega y Gasset who lived centuries later than Socrates, but who was similarly committed to self-understanding, writes:[2]

Our essential character is reflected in our prayers

"There is a true religious attitude at the center of the urge to understand, and, as far as I am concerned, I must confess that, when I get up in the morning, I recite a very brief prayer, thousand of years old, a verse from the *Rig-Veda*, which contains these few winged words:

"Lord, awaken us in a happy mood and give us knowledge!"

Thus prepared, I go through the bright or gloomy hours that come with the day.

These sages tell us that there is a way in which we shape the nature of our own longings. It is by assuming a degree of responsibility for our lives at their centers. This is something we neglect in an age of super-surface excitement and peripheral vision.

How is it that one person—old, young, middleaged—age doesn't really make much difference—preserves the impulse to look for beauty within and without? How is it that we go up and down, one day feeling ourselves full of good potentials and the next day feeling bound and imprisoned by hard circumstances? And what does all this have to do with willing and choosing?

Of primary importance is our posture to the day as it begins, and to our universe and to ourselves. True strength begins, I believe, as we learn that within us there are potentials for growth, resources of the mind and spirit which are not fabricated by human intelligence or ingenuity, but are there in us to be uncovered, discovered, nourished and opened up, but not to be invented.

We are taught this by teachers like Socrates and Ortega. Their "findings" are also being offered by certain contemporary psychologists who speak of our need to discover or uncover the good that is in us. We cannot *create* that "good," though we can establish conditions which make it more possible for it to manifest itself. These words of Abraham Maslow are to the point:[3]

> "Even though 'weak,' this inner nature rarely disappears or dies, in the usual person, in the U.S. (such disappearance or dying is possible early in the life history, however.) It persists underground, unconsciously, even though denied and repressed. Like the voice of the intellect (which is part of it), it speaks softly but it will be heard, even if in a distorted form. That is, it has a dynamic force of its own pressing always for open, uninhibited expression. Effort must be used in its suppression or repression from which fatigue can result. This force is one main aspect of the 'will to health'...."

Maslow holds that the nature of our inner nature is basically and intrinsically good though subject to sickness and distortion, and in its creativity weaker than certain instinctual needs, weaker, that is, in its initial phases. He holds that these impulses of ours toward creativity and beauty, though they are weak, do not often disappear completely.

It strikes me that our inner self—our "intentionality"—is like certain vines that have a powerful way of coming back after forest fires. I recall a house in a bombed out section of the city of Mannheim, Germany. Mannheim was 70% destroyed during the second World War and I lived in it for a good many months before it was rebuilt. This particular house had been bombed and gutted by fire. I used to drive by it almost daily in the spring of 1945. I watched a wisteria vine growing and became involved in its struggle for life. Over the weeks it persisted in climbing over the ruins and finally it blossomed as though there were in it a capacity to blossom which would not be denied by bombs and fire.

I find it helpful to keep in mind these five inner-nature assumptions of Maslow's.[4]

1. "We have, each of us, an essential inner nature, which is to some degree 'natural,' intrinsic, given, and, in a certain sense, unchangeable, or, at least, unchanging.

2. Each person's nature is in part unique to himself and in part species-wide.

3. It is possible to study this inner nature scientifically and to discover what it is like—not *invent, discover*.

4. This inner nature, as much as we know of it so far, seems not to be intrinsically evil, but rather either neutral or positively "good." What we call evil appears most often to be a secondary reaction to frustration of this intrinsic nature.

5. Since this inner nature is good rather than bad, it is best to bring it out and to encourage it, rather than to suppress it. If it is permitted to guide our life, we grow healthy, fruitful and happy.

And I would add to these five points his warning with respect to self-deception, and even self-hatred:[5]

> "The serious thing for each person to recognize vividly and poignantly, each for himself, is that every falling away from species-virtue, every crime against one's own nature, every evil act, *every one without exception*, records itself in our unconscious and makes us despise ourselves."

I think Maslow is offering us a personal credo—substantiated also by other "third force" psychologists[5] which is based on empirical evidence gathered from the lives of his patients and gathered from his own life. He is unusual in that he made a point of concentrating on the nature of health rather than the nature of sickness.

In the traditions of religious humanism we have the same credo offered in different languages and symbols.

Here it is in words attributed to the Buddha:

Be ye lamps unto yourself.
Be your own reliance.
Hold to the truth within yourselves as to the only lamp.

Here it is in the Hindu literature:

Thou are the path and the goal that paths never reach.
Thou feedest or sustainest all that man sees or seems.
Thou are the trembling grass and the tiger that creeps under it.

Thou art the light in sun and moon, the sounds fading into silence, the sanctity of sacred books—the good that destroys evil.

Here it is in the Old Testament:

Then I said, I will not make mention of him, nor speak any more in his name, but his word was in my heart as a burning fire shut up in my bones, and I was weary with forbearing, and I could not stay (refrain from speaking). Jeremiah.

In Jeremiah it is the prophetic voice which speaks in these days through Martin Luther King, Robert Kennedy, Malcolm X, Eldridge Cleaver and so many others. All these persons know the impulse, the longing for social justice as a fire in their bones which they did not kindle and which they cannot extinguish.

Oscar Wilde calls this inner reality "humility." I think it might also be thought of as a deep kind of pride in one's own life and self, but Oscar Wilde's words are beautifully descriptive:

"Now I find hidden somewhere away in my nature something that tells me nothing in the whole world is meaningless, and my suffering least of all. That something hidden away in my nature, like a treasure in a field, is humility.

"It is the last thing left in me and the best... the ultimate *discovery* at which I have arrived, the starting point for a fresh development. It has come to me right out of myself, so that I know it has come at the proper time ... It is the one thing that has in it all the elements of life, of a new life, a new way for me. Of all things it is the strangest; One cannot give it away and another may not give it to one. One cannot acquire it, except by surrendering everything that one has. It is only when one has lost all things that one possesses it."

What does all this have to do with willing and choosing?

I would make two observations: In our willing and choosing we are involved in a paradox, inescapably so. True strength of will is contingent upon our wisdom, to perceive that what is given to us is written into our natures. We did not put it there any more that we put into the universe its mysterious potential for differing forms of life. We can block it, stymie it, frustrate it, and it is at least an open question as to whether we can destroy it permanently, though we are very clever in our destructiveness. But my point is, that it is in some sense "given"—*discovered*, not *invented*.

This must be one of the meanings back of the words so often used at traditional burial service, words which grate on the modern desire to be always in control, never dependent: "The Lord giveth, the Lord taketh away, blessed by the name of the Lord."

The second observation I would make is: that which is given by God, by life, by the universe, by ... you name it ... is somehow in a contingent relationship to us. We have to bring it to birth each day by consciously cultivated acts of choice, by acts of will, by deliberately confronting ourselves and others, by the posture with which we deliberately confront each new day.

Buddhist wisdom tells us that hatred does not cease by hatred, only by love. We have to *choose* love over an over again in order to make an end to hatred in ourselves and in others.

"Behold I set before you life and death." We *can* choose life— we can also choose death.

The Kingdom of God is within us. We can choose whether or not it will come through us and be actualized in the world around us.

The New Testament puts it, "Look you are the children of God and it does not yet appear what you shall be." I take it that this means that the potential for good is given whether or not it is actualized is up to us.

Again insights from Abraham Maslow are corroborative:[6]

"However, this inner core, or self, grows into adulthood only partly by (objective or subjective) discovery, uncovering and acceptance of what is "there" beforehand. Partly it is also a creation of the person himself. Life is a continual series of choices for the individual in which a main determinant of choice is the person as he already is (including his goals for himself, his courage or fear, his feeling of responsibility, his ego-strength or "will power," etc.) We can no longer think of the person as "fully determined" where this phrase implies "determined only by forces external to the person." The person, insofar as he is a real person, is his own main determinant. Every person is, in part, 'his own project' and makes himself."

I started with the prayer of Socrates because I wanted to illustrate that prayer, wishing and projecting are deeply related to willing and choosing. I will close with it but preface it with another prayer which is also highly meaningful.

We need not get hung up on the theological terminology if we remember that what we are concerned with here is on the one hand the reality of the good potential which is in us and on the other the power of the will to serve as midwife to and nourisher of the good.

Fix thou our steps, O Lord, that we stagger not at the uneven motions of the world, but go steadily on our way, neither censuring our journey for the weather we meet, nor turning aside for anything that befalls us.

***

Beloved Pan, and ye other gods that haunt this place, give us beauty in the inward soul; and may the outward and inward be at one. May I reckon the wise to be wealthy, and may I have such a quantity of gold as none but the temperate can carry.

*****

NOTES

1. Rollo May, *Love and Will*, W.W. Norton C., Inc., 1969, p. 81. His words prefatory to the prayer are worth noting.

2. José Ortega y Gasset, *Meditations on Don Quixote*, pp. 37-38.

3. Abraham H. Maslow, *Toward a Psychology of Being*, p. 180, D. Van Nostrand Co., Inc., 1962.

4. Abraham H. Maslow, *The Self*, Harper and Row, 1956, editor, Clark E. Moustakis, pp 232, 233, 234.

5. Abraham H. Maslow, *Toward a Psychology of Being*, D. Van Nostrand Co., Inc. See p. viii for a description of the "Third Force."

6. Abraham H. Maslow, *idem*, pp 180-181.

GROWING TOWARD PERSONHOOD III

"ATTENTION IS I-CAN"

What does it mean to be attentive—*to pay attention*? It means to become aware of worlds we have not really known existed. It means to cross the threshold of those worlds and to enter into their realness. They may be worlds of pleasure. They may be worlds of pain and suffering. The thresholds may be vocational or avocational. In either event they can lead to worlds whose existence we had only suspected.

Years ago I read a story about the noted sportswriter, John Kieran. He told the story on himself. He was a young man teaching school in upstate New York. Someone interested him in ornithology, the science of *paying attention* to birds. Suddenly a new world opened up around him. It was spring of the year and he became aware that the very world in which he had been sleeping and waking and walking and breathing was brimming musically and visually with creatures of whom up to that point he had had only the most inattentive kind of awareness. He awoke, and from that time on he embraced another universe, or another part of the one universe, which had been closed to him.

Emerson puts it beautifully: *Our eyes are holden that we cannot see the things that stare us in the face until the time arrives when the mind is opened, then the time when we saw them not is a dream.*

The act of *paying* attention—note the commercial metaphor—is what today is called *being turned on*. If we think that paying attention is inevitably an active phenomenon, we are leaving out part of the picture. How large a part I am not sure. Not infrequently a friend will say to us, "I'm glad I *got* your attention." He is saying quite accurately that he had as much to do with *getting* our attention as we did with *giving* it. There is reality in the passive state of the phrase, *being turned on*. But whether we give our attention or whether we capture another person's attention, there is a good deal to Simone Weil's observation that the greatest of human capacities is the capacity for attention.

The history of a word tells us a lot about its layers of meaning. Attention comes from the Latin word *attendere* which means 'to stretch.' So we can say, to begin with, that there is a stretching quality to being attentive. We stretch our faculties to relate ourselves to that which is outside ourselves—also to that which is inside ourselves, but which is neither perceived or felt without conscious stretching.

When the French Phenomenologist, Merleau-Ponty, says that "every intention is attention and attention is I-can," he means that to which we are really paying attention is that in which we are actually involved.[1] Attention eventually becomes action, otherwise it is pseudo. I think he also means, and here he relates attention to intention, that the action is more than a surface phenomenon.

Full attention flows from the deeper *willing* part of our natures. It is not idle fancy or phantasy, though fancy and phantasy may represent a foreshadowing of it. It is a current that flows from our center and may be the growth-product of many years. It is rooted in both the conscious and unconscious levels of our being.

I have become more interested in recent years in instances of accomplishment which appear to have come out of the blue without any prior warning or indication. It may be a singular achievement in human relationships. The *isolated* quality of the event tends to disappear as we learn more about the doer,—the accomplisher. With more knowledge of the person, what at first looked so spectacularly isolated now appears to be a natural development of sequences well-rooted in that person's life style and orientation.

There is another significant element in the derivation of the word *attention*. If it has the meaning to *stretch*, to *reach out*, it also has the connotation of *tending* or *caring for*. Caring is an especially precious kind of life faculty by no means limited to humans but flowering in humanness in rare and enduring ways. In its finer reaches *being attentive to* is caring for, is being loving. Robert Frost observed that in the fall of the year or in the winter a farmer—he probably did this himself—would stroll into the woods and break off a bit of branch from a sleeping tree and handle it "tenderlike." We can see the derivative link between at*tend* and "*tend*erlike." It is not merely *stretching*, it is also *caring*, *tending*, that brings into the act of attention a quality of love. Attention is as much a function of the heart as of the mind.

> *Caring is an especially precious kind of life faculty by no means limited to humans*

In all I am saying I am not unmindful of the fact that attention may also be permeated by hate.

In his recent book, *Love and Will*, a significant book which has much in it that is not easy to grasp, Rollo May has much to say about *intentionality*. He attempts a number of descriptions. He describes it as the "structure which gives meaning to experience." (n. 2, pp. 223-224) It is "the constructive use of normal anxiety ... without intentionality we are indeed 'nothing'." (n. 3, p. 244) He agrees with Paul Tillich that intentionality, vitality and courage go together. (n. 4, p. 244) The same is true of intentionality and caring. (n. 5, p. 292) He links intentionality to the "unconscious." (n. 6, p. 234) He decries artificial separation of the intention and the act. (n. 7, p. 242)

The concept is obviously a hard one to put into words even for a thinker as articulate as Rollo May. But as I think about what he writes—and I think of my intentionality—and as I relate it to my own thinking and feeling, my own being, it seems to me that intentionality lies back of, and is indeed the cradle of our human capacity at one and the same time the paradoxical realness of our own individuality and our oneness with both the world and with other human beings.

Sometimes we curse ourselves and are bitterly frustrated because we can't pay attention to the goals we have chosen, or that we think we have chosen. But it may be that the goal we pursue is not really *our* goal in the sense that we want it wholly and profoundly. We may be embracing it and rejecting it at the same time. At a conscious level we say, "Yes." At other levels of self-awareness we say, "No." If we are able to pursue it, it may be only at the price of denying the more creative, the fun and enjoying part of ourselves.

> *Sometimes we can't pay attention to the goals we have chosen, or that we think we have chosen*

I think it is Erich Fromm who tells of a man who came to him for psychotherapy. He was desperately unhappy. It developed that he was trying with might and main to force himself to go into his father's business though he wanted to be an artist, or perhaps it was a teacher. Struggling with the decision, he had about made up his mind that he himself wanted to do what his father wanted him to do. Then he dreamed. In the dream he is driving a car down a twisting, narrow mountain road. He comes to a fork in the road. His impulses are to go in one direction, but he fights his impulses and goes in another direction. He drives a short while and is confronted with a sheer precipice. He is able to stop the car, but had his brakes not held, he would have plunged over the cliff, killing himself and those who were with him. Subsequently, he decided that despite his father's strong wishes, he must *pay attention* to his own inner voice. He stretches toward himself. He cares for himself.

He knows that to live by his own voice will not be easy. But it is the way. Not to pay attention to himself, to reach toward himself, to care for himself is to court self-destruction.

I am making the point that attention is not a spasmodic act, something we tack on to ourselves. At its deepest it grows out of our total intentionality. It is not going somewhere casually—though it has very large margins of spontaneity because it is a product of the whole person. It includes play and phantasy as well as the rational. It is willing to go somewhere with both mind and heart—responsibly, responsibly with our whole beings. It involves spontaneity and also disciplined commitment. It involves living in the present but also stretching toward the future. It means entering into life with laughter, but it involves also the knowledge that laughter and tears are often very close together.

Attention is I-can, writes Merleau-Ponty. To me this means that attention fully given, changes the world, opens doors to new worlds, leads us to fresh understandings of old worlds. It is my conviction, for example, that when I pay attention to defeat, it may cease to be defeat, at least, in any *dead-end* sense. I think I know from personal experience something of what these words of William Carlos Williams mean:

> *No defeat is made up entirely of defeat—since*
> *the world it opens is always a place*
> > *formerly*
> > > *unsuspected. A*
>
> *world lost,*
> > *a world unsuspected,*
> > > *beckons to new places.*

But we have to pay *careful, stretching* attention to our defeats to be able to see and to be able to enter into the new places they may conceal. Sometimes it is only long after the difficult event that we come to see how we were led by it, and through it, to new places which would have remained unknown had we not crossed painful thresholds.

Attention is not to take either defeat or victory for granted. In fact it is to take nothing for granted but to remain open continuously to recurring possibilities for growth and the recurring reality of the world's wonder.

Attention is the flowering of the Spirit.

Attention is the capacity to see extraordinary possibilities in ordinary situations. Indeed, attention says, "If you pay attention closely you will see that there is nothing ordinary about the ordinary."

Attention enables us to turn death situations into life situations. Emily Dickinson said it.

A Death-blow is a life-blow to some
Who, till they died, did not alive become;
Who had they lived, had died, but when
They died, vitality begun.

"Attention is I-can."

*****

NOTES

1. Rollo May, *Love and Will*, W.W. Norton Co. Inc, 1969.

May quotes Merleau-Ponty, "That is, 'every intention is an attention, and attention is I-can,' as Merleau Ponty puts it. We are, therefore, unable to give attention to something until we are able to experience an 'I-can' with regard to it." p. 232.

2. *Love and Will*, pp. 223, 225,

"By intentionality, I mean the structure which gives meaning to experience. It is not to be identified with intentions, but it is the dimension which underlies them. It is our imaginative participation is the coming day's possibilities."

3. *Love and Will*, p. 244,

"Intentionality is the constructive use of normal anxiety. If I can have some expectations and possibility of acting on my own powers, I move ahead, but if the anxiety becomes overwhelming, then the possibilities for action are blocked out. Thus Paul Tillich points out that pronounced neurotic anxiety destroys intentionality."

4. *Love and Will*, p. 244,

"Tillich goes on, interestingly enough, to relate intentionality to vitality, and then to courage: 'man's vitality is as great as his intentionality: they are interdependent. This makes man the most vital of all beings. He can transcend any given situation in any direction and this possibility drives him to create beyond himself.'"

5. *Love and Will*, p. 292,

"The common, original meaning of 'intentionality' and 'care' lies in the little term 'tend' which is both the root of intentionality and the meaning of care."

6. *Love and Will*, p. 234,

"Intentionality, as I am using the term, goes below levels of immediate awareness, and includes spontaneous, bodily elements and other dimensions which are usually called 'unconscious'."

7. *Love and Will*, p. 242,

"The separation of intention and act is an artificial posture and does not accurately describe human experience. The act is in the intention, and the intention is the act."

GROWING TOWARD PERSONHOOD IV

NOTES ON INNER SPACE TRAVEL

Today we are occupied with outer space. The recent flights to the moon have excited our imaginations. They have affected our image of the earth. It is important to remember that the image we have of the earth shapes the image we have of ourselves. Any conception of self or personhood which is not rooted in a widening view of cosmos is stunted and static. Our image of our cosmos and our self-image go hand-in-hand. They grow together.

Archibald MacLeish made this point with great sensitivity in his reflection on the flight of Apollo VIII. He tells us that the sight of the earth seen by the astronauts from the depths of space—and literally seen by us through their eyes—may mark the beginning of a new relationship between man and the earth.[1]

> "Men's conception of themselves and of each other has always depended on their notion of the earth.... Now in the last few days, the notion may have changed again. For the first time in all of time men have seen the earth: seen it not as continents or oceans from the little distance of a hundred miles or two or three, but seen it from the depths of space; seen it whole and round and beautiful and small as even Dante—that "first imagination of Christendom"—had never dreamed of seeing it; as the twentieth century philosophers of absurdity and despair were incapable of guessing that it might be seen. And seeing

it so, one question came to the minds of those who looked at it. "Is it inhabited?" they said to each other and laughed—and then they did not laugh. What came to their minds a hundred thousand miles and more into space—"half way to the moon" they put it—lonely, floating planet: that tiny raft in the enormous, empty night. "Is it inhabited?"

"The Medieval notion of the earth put man at the center of everything. The nuclear notion of the earth put him nowhere—beyond the range of reason even—lost in absurdity and war. This latest notion may have other consequences. Formed as it was in the minds of heroic voyagers who were also men, it may remake our image of mankind. No longer that preposterous figure at the center, no longer that degraded and degrading victim off at the margins of reality and blind with blood, man may at last become himself.

"To see the earth as it truly is, small and blue and beautiful in that eternal silence where it floats, is to see ourselves as riders on the earth together, brothers on that bright loveliness in the eternal cold—brothers who know that they are truly brothers."

Everything in this sidereal universe is mysterious and wonderful. Everything is a puzzlement. It is only when we shut ourselves up in our cocoons of "absolute" knowledge—only when we have wrapped ourselves in limiting dogmas—"scientific" as well as religious—that we can define ourselves with spurious comfort and security.

Inner space is no less mysterious and wonder-full than outer space. As images of the universe change with increasing human experience, questioning and exploration, so do images of the self. Any narrow definition of the inner life, whether it comes from learned psychologists or from theologians or from popular thinking, is a snare and a delusion. If I tell you too certainly who I am, what my personhood is, what my inner life is,—in the very moment I tell you that which it truly is slips away, like a stream of quietly moving water, or a bit of quick silver. What I thought was pigeon holed has already flown the coop.

It is as much a piece of folly to try to define the self in an absolute sense as it is to try to give a static definition of God. I am uneasy whenever I meet anybody who puts God in a basket and claims to be able to deliver him-her-it *on order* as though deity were a parcel of groceries. I am also uneasy at those who describe God in such generalities that unlike good groceries she-he-it has no *particular* taste, flavor, smell, sweetness or bitterness. With regard to what self or personhood is— we do well to recall Meister Eckhart's almost mocking words about God: "Whatever you say He is, He is not. And whatever you say He is not, He is."

> *I am uneasy whenever I meet anybody who puts God in a basket*

Our exterior world, the world of stars and planets, trees and wind and water, the world of molecules and mountain ranges is indissolubly linked to our inner world. All existence underscores the fact of the interdependence of outer and inner worlds. As a matter of fact, we only divide the world into "inner" and "outer" for purposes of description and reflection. It has been said that if the population of New York, San Francisco or any large city lost all memory of the past, within a matter of weeks, 80% of the population would be dead. So the past is related to the present and so our very survival depends on what is "in our heads."

It is true that the quality of life we live is dependent upon the care we give to the terrestrial universe, upon our concern for what is outside of us. It is equally true that the quality of the life we live is dependent upon what goes on within us, with our concern for inner space.

We are well aware now that there are indispensable rules for travel in outer space. I have forgotten the total sum of countdown points that are enumerated before any space craft, with its cargo of astronauts, leaves the earth's surface. Are there similar count-down points, embodying accumulated knowledge, which should be checked out for inner space exploration? There are guidelines for travel in inner space—insights, bits of wisdom which have been accumulated over the millennia out of the experiences of those who have sought to travel and explore within themselves. Much of it adds up to the essence of the wisdom of great religious teachings. In our times it is also a significant and hopeful happening that men and women of science are exploring inner space with a growing appreciation of the importance of the experience of the religious ones, the seers and the mystics.[2]

There are guidelines for travel in inner space—insights, bits of wisdom

I would like to make some observations about inner space. These observations are based on much reading on and study of the subject. Most of all, they are based on some inner-space trips which I myself have taken.

Inner space is filled with all sorts of people and non-people. There was a picture of the Apollo VIII astronauts on the moon's surface in which a curious light effect made it appear that one of them was being shadowed, followed or even haunted by some spectral or astral form. Inner space is a place of memory, feeling, wish and will, of recollection and anticipation. It, too, is filled with people real and imagined. Sometimes these inhabitants are seen clearly. Sometimes they are very much distorted so that looking inward we see a gathering of ghosts. These people are tremendous sources of health and wholeness. Our inner space would be frightfully barren and quite terrifyingly empty without them.

Our inner space is inhabited not only by people but by things, all kind of things. About 100 or 150 yards from the house in which I grew up there was a great flat rock, perhaps as much as twenty by ten feet, which was striped by very clear glacial markings. That rock is there in my inner space. It is a significant inhabitant. Lo, these many years it has reminded me of the antiquity of the earth and of the dependence of our existence upon glacial forces beyond our control. I think that for me it is a great paradoxical symbol of permanence and impermanence.

In my childhood there was a river which had a bend in it. It flows now in my inner space. Mark Twain, who was brought up in Hannibal, Missouri, where the great Mississippi River turns and moves off into the horizon, thought that every child's life should have a river with a bend in it, giving the child intimations of distance, and movement beyond the horizon. My river still takes me beyond distant horizons.

In my childhood, not far from the house where I lived, there were three great elm trees. They had a dignity and a beauty which spoke to me. Those three trees spoke from my inner space the other day when I saw Rembrandt's etching *The Three Trees*. I also think of them when every Christmas I read T.S. Eliot's lines in *The Journey of the Magi*.

> *"Then at dawn we came down to a temperate valley*
> *Wet below the snowline, smelling of vegetation:*
> *With a running stream and a water mill beating the darkness,*
> *And three trees on the low sky,*
> *And an old white horse galloped away in the meadow."*

But in addition to the rocks and the trees and the rivers, the city streets, the flat plains, the mountains and the seas, there are in inner space, people who have a potent influence for hope or for despair — in the present as in time past. The world of inner space abrogates the laws of time, so that past and present and future, too, are the same. So the inhabitants of that world are as near to us now as they were so many years ago.

How do we become what we are? It is a matter of outward circumstances in part. But outward circumstances have a way of translating themselves into inner realities, and sometimes it is very hard to say where the "outer" ends and where the "inner" begins. Ask people where they get their qualities of independence, their zest for adventure, their deep anxieties. The answer is likely to come back in words like these: "You see, I had this teacher in anthropology, and he opened doors".... "I had this uncle, he was what you might call an odd ball, but he was a wonderful person".... "My father and mother, they were always helping us be ourselves, encouraging us to try new ways, to do the things we ourselves really wanted to do."

Another person may change our life direction not only by what he says or does but also by what he or she is inwardly. The state of his or her inner space communicates itself to us and changes us.

"I had intended to major in mathematics, but a biology teacher changed my mind. He was a wonderful man with one of the finest philosophies of life I had ever known. Even in class he would bring out things of a moral nature. He was a man of high character and showed us the origin and meaning of life."[3]

Into our inner world flow currents of strength and hope and courage from the inner worlds of others. Inner worlds are as surely interdependent and as surely nourish one another as plants are nourished by soil and sun and rain. People who have lived in the past, people who live in the present—people with whom our lot is cast day in, day out, year in, year out—all these illumine and strengthen us. Time does not seem to be of the essence here. Influence—which means in-flowing - may come slowly over many patient years, or dramatically like a flash of light in the dark. I believe we can never think deeply about our inner life without being thankful that it has been open to, and touched by the inner life of others.

Into our inner world flow currents

I would not want to leave the impression that our inner space is inhabited only by "good" people and "good" happenings. As a matter of fact, when I began to think about my inner space, I started from a negative bias. The thoughts that came to me were on the nightmarish aspect of inwardness, the concentration of fears and even terror that can be a part of inwardness. But gradually I moved toward a more hopeful stance. I did this consciously because I wanted to focus on positive experiences of inwardness. The horrors of the inner life are real enough, the barrenness and fear—sometimes. But I wanted to underscore Ortega's insight:[4]

> "What we today receive already decorated with sublime aureoles once had to contract and shrink in order to pass through a man's heart. All that is recognized today as truth, as perfect beauty, as highly valuable, was once born in the inner spirit of an individual, mixed with his whims and humors.

When we experience our "inner spirit" we know that we are peopled by those whose lives and beings have flowed up, over and into our own. Not only persons but places, atmospheres—small and large galaxies of precious experiences. They are all part of us. When we travel in our inner space, we know that life backs up against life. There are flowing springs. There is a creative spirit, an affirmative spirit, even in the midst of desolation.

There is a creativity that does not die though it changes its colour and its feeling and motion as time passes, and we go through life cycles of life and death. Though there are many persons in our inner space, there is no person who has ever seen exactly what we have seen, or experienced what we have experienced. We know that we are at the same time and at one with all humanity. We are aware that the inner space which is ours is a mysterious source of wonder, and that when it has gone dry it is not because it has ceased to exist: it is because we have ceased to exist. It is not because others have ceased to be: it is because we have become blind to their nearness and dulled to their richness. Our inner spaces have ceased to touch one another.

There is a creativity that does not die though it changes its colour and its feeling and motion

Some twelve years ago Dag Hammarskjold wrote these lines.[5] They are cast in a theistic mold, but that should not throw us off. The

United Nations Secretary General puts the truth in his words—we must put it in our own words.

"God does not die on the day when we cease to believe in a personal deity, but we die on the day when our lives cease to be illumined by the steady radiance, renewed daily, of a wonder, the source of which is beyond all reason."

My own words go like this:

"The well is full, whatever made you think it wasn't?
The spring still flows, what made you think it had gone dry?
The inner space is filled with music, with what noises have
you cut yourself off from the melody?
The inner space is filled with hope and courage,
what terror have you allowed to stand between you and its
light?

While Tagore puts it this way:

The time that my journey takes is long and the way of it
long.
I came out on the chariot of the first gleam of light, and
pursued my voyage through the wilderness of worlds
leaving my track on many a star and planet.
It is the most distant course that comes nearest to thyself,
and that training is the most intricate which leads to the
utter simplicity of a tune.
The traveller has to knock at every alien door to come to his
own, and one has to wander through all the outer worlds to
reach the innermost shrine and the end.
My eyes strayed far and wide before I shut them and said,
"Here are thou!"
The question and the cry, "Oh, where?" melt into tears of a

thousand streams and deluge the world with the flood of assurance "I am!"

*****

NOTES

1. Quoted from an article in *Look* Magazine on the Flight of Apollo 8 by Archibald MacLeish.

2. I recommend Abraham Maslow's writings for the development of this point, particularly his *Religions, Values, and Peak Experiences*, Ohio State University Press, 1964.

3. *Fourteen Journeys to Unitarianism*, as told to Jeannette Hopkins, Beacon Press, 1954.

4. *Meditations on Quixote* by José Ortega y Gasset, W.W. Norton and Company, 1961, pp. 43, 44.

5. *Markings* by Dag Hammarskjold, Alfred A. Knopf, p. 56.

LET THE CONGREGATIONS SPEAK

I would speak this morning on the relationship of the church to public issues. Let us bear in mind the fact that on March 18th this congregation will be holding a meeting at which we, as church members, will be asked by our Social Action Committee and our Board of Trustees to discuss and to make known our views on two of the controversial issues of the day: the issue of shelters and the issue of nuclear testing. Although it has been customary in recent years for our National Assembly and for regional meetings of our denomination to take stands on issues of this sort, which represent at least the views of the delegates present and voting, it is somewhat unusual for a local church to follow this procedure; so in a sense we are acting, I am proud to say, in a pioneer role.

many questions arise when a church seeks to pioneer

There are always many questions which arise when a church seeks to pioneer. Among the questions which arise in the minds of men and women devoted to the welfare and development of this church are such questions as these: Is it wise for a congregation, as a congregation, to take a stand on a public issue? Of what value, in the total context of the society, is a stand, once it is taken? What of the disagreement within the congregation which is likely to be engendered in this delicate process? Should a church seek to deal with moral and social issues in general terms, leaving the application of specifics to the individual church member? Certainly, this is a traditional approach in American Protestantism, and it calls to mind a story which is dear to the hearts of ministers, a story of a minister who was invited to candidate for the pulpit of a church in the southern part of the United States. He preached twice. His first sermon title was "Thou shall Not Steal." The sermon made a great impression on the people, and they were extremely enthusiastic about it. When he came back the second Sunday, he took for his title "Thou Shalt Not Steal Chickens." On this occasion he was lucky to escape with his life! The story reflects a dilemma which is not peculiar to southern churches and not peculiar to the application of this single commandment.

The problems with which we are seeking to wrestle a congregation are by no means unique to our situation; they are the problems of many thoughtful men and women who are concerned with the future of the churches and the future of organized religion in this country. In recent years the Fund for the Republic has published two studies in this field, embodying the points of view of able men representing Judaism, Catholicism and Protestantism. William Lee Miller, a theologian at the Yale Divinity School, wrote one of these studies.[1] I would commend it to you because it deals in an unusually candid way with both the strengths and the weaknesses of the churches. I have found from personal experience in recent months, serving as a member of the Unitarian Universalist National Commission on Ethics and Social Action, that certainly there are denominations in the country which can teach us a good deal in this area. The Quakers are one of those denominations, and the Methodists are another. We should be ready to learn from those who have advanced beyond ourselves in making religion more relevant to our times.

> *thoughtful men and women are concerned with the future of the churches*

Let us look briefly at the history of our church, the First Unitarian Church of San Francisco. I am especially conscious of our history this morning because I had an invitation to visit the office building located at 133 Geary Street. Those of you who are historically minded will recall that this was the site of the church built in San Francisco in 1864, under the leadership of Thomas Starr King. As you walk into the hallway of the building, you see a bronze plaque. That plaque reminded me that it was 98 years ago today, on March 4, 1864, that Thomas Starr King died. We are celebrating an anniversary.

look briefly at the history of our church

Starr King was in this community for four years. In that four years he accomplished an incredible amount of work and released throughout the state an incredible amount of social idealism. Tragically, he had the opportunity to preach only seven times in his new church when death overtook him at the age of 39. But during his brief ministry in California, a symbol of the relevance of private religious concerns to public social issues. Because he became so great a symbol, the city was draped in mourning on the day of his funeral, and by order of the Federal Government, the guns on Alcatraz sounded a memorial tribute.

We need in this church no reminder of what a single individual can do when he is committed. Thomas Starr King was chiefly responsible for California's magnificent contribution of one and a half million dollars to the Sanitary commission, forerunner of the American Red Cross, which ministered to the men wounded on Civil War battlefields. If my memory is accurate, this million and a half dollars was the largest amount contributed by any single state. Thomas Starr King, of course, is known even more for his efforts on behalf of the Union. Following the Confederacy's attack on Fort Sumter, he did more than any other single citizen to persuade the State of California to the cause of freedom and to the cause of the Union. So we have in Thomas Starr King a signal example of the way in which social idealism and personal religious conviction can be fused in a single individual, and through this process of fusion can influence the destiny of a people in ways almost beyond belief.

A carpenter was once called in to shingle the roof of a little New England church. He had difficulty with one of the deacons of the church who had swindled him in several business deals. The carpenter swore that, tucked up among the shingles of the church's roof, he found all the prayers that the deacon had ever uttered in the sanctuary; they had never gotten beyond the roof! If Starr King's church were still standing at 133 Geary Street and a carpenter were called into re-shingle the roof, he would not find there a single prayer of Thomas Starr King. Because his religion bound him together as one whole person, his prayers went as far up and farther than did John Glenn a few days ago!

We note that his social idealism came from the center of his being. He was not concerned with the peripheral political activities of his generation. He lived from the center out, and his abiding faith *the ancient words of Micah come to life* in the deep, lasting moral values was so strong that wherever it touched political expediency and political issues, it lifted those issues beyond the area of partisanship and made the ancient words of Micah come to life: "What doth the Lord require of thee but to do justly and to love mercy and to walk humbly with thy God."

No detailed study of the relationship of the relationship of Thomas Starr King to his San Francisco congregation has been made which is similar in depth to the study recently made of one of his contemporaries and friends, the great abolitionist minister, William Henry Furness, who served the Unitarian Church in Philadelphia. It would be instructive to know if these two men had identical relationships to their congregations. I suspect there were differences between San Francisco and Philadelphia in that day, perhaps even more marked that they are on this day. The study of Furness's ministry shows that although there was a strong, dissident majority opposed to his social idealism, some of whom withdrew from the church under rather dramatic conditions, most of the congregation stood with him, as apparently the whole congregation of Starr Kind stood with him. The study in Philadelphia also shows the significant fact that there was a marked tendency on the part of the congregation to let the minister speak to the social issues, to support him to the full in his brave and thoughtful endeavors, but to take no action on social issues as a congregation or as a church.

Today in Unitarian and Universalist circles, and this is true of other denominations, we seem to be moving into another dimension of religious expression. We seem to be concerned that out of the church congregation itself there shall come study procedures, meetings, and finally a voice through which the congregation shall make known its own commitment to ideal values. This process does not mean that the individual member of the congregation will cease to act primarily in his religious capacity as an individual. It does not mean that the individualism of the minister, so greatly honored and encouraged in our tradition, will become less marked. It does mean that our liberal congregations will slowly learn to discipline themselves to speak for themselves; and it does mean that certain conditions must be fulfilled if this speaking is to be effective and wise. It means, for example, that the issues on which there is a voice raised must be carefully chosen in terms of their genuine and deep relevance to religious concerns. It means that what is narrowly partisan and political must be avoided as the plague. It means that the process of study and preparation going into any consideration of public issues must be serious and well-planned, as serious and as well-planned as the procedures adopted by our own Social Action Committee as it has sought in recent months to challenge us to think through the issues of shelters and nuclear testing. It means that, as a religious community, we have to learn to discipline ourselves to accept disagreement without bitterness, for there will be disagreement.

One of the arguments which is raised against a congregation taking a stand on a controversial issue is that the congregation is likely to disagree and become divided. Unity in the face of diversity is hard to achieve. The discipline achieved by the Quaker movement, with its magnificent social idealism, is the fruit of four centuries of life and experience. Before a Quaker Meeting speaks as a Meeting, consensus is required. I am told that sometimes a single, dissenting individual will block the voice of the Meeting for months, or perhaps for years.

Unity in the face of diversity is hard to achieve

Our church has approximately one thousand members, representing every kind of political position and a tremendous variety of theological viewpoints. It will not be easy for us to speak as a congregation. To do so will require a degree of work and patience which will try us deeply. To face disagreement and benefit by it takes wisdom; and wisdom does not come cheaply. I predict that if we follow this line of development, we will meet many problems that we do not now foresee. I predict further that some of the problems which now appear to be insoluble, such as the problem of disagreement and division, will prove to be soluble as we learn to face them together in a broad and constructive spirit.

As Americans, we have strange expectations of our churches. We have, for example, the unrealistic expectation of perfection. We expect that when the minister speaks, he speaks, as it were, as the Pope speaks—*ex cathedra*, from the chair, infallibly—and that it cannot be his prerogative or the prerogative of the church to be wrong. We have a tendency to segregate the church from all other forms of institutions, to consider it holy in an absolutely unique sense. We say that there must be no disagreement within the church; it must speak with a single voice. So we forget that the church is essentially a human institution and that its task is to be holy not in the sense that God is holy, but to be "holy in the human sense." We forget that the church cannot speak with a single voice, nor can it speak infallibly, because it is made up of human beings who are fallible. We must learn to recognize this, and we must learn to think of the church humbly, as a workshop in which we face and even profit from our theological disagreements and our disagreements in social philosophy.

We have the feeling that the church must always be above politics. So it must, if politics are construed in a narrow sense. But this does not mean that the church should not be soiled by the dirt of the day, or disturbed by the day's tensions. To keep the church out of the arena of our deepest social concern is, to say the least, an exercise in ambivalence. On the one side, it seems to imply deep reverence; on the other side, it makes the church irrelevant in the name of absolute purity, holiness and virtue. It puts the church on a shelf and keeps it silent when it should speak out. I grant you that a congregation is indeed likely to look foolish when it debates and takes stands on issues on which the most brilliant of men disagree. This is true. But it is also true that it is better for a church to look foolish, to look "impractically idealistic," than to be irrelevant. It should be a sobering thought to us that no group looked more foolish in the first century to the officials of the Roman Empire than Jesus and has small group of disciples. It should be a sobering thought that history has frequently shown a strange predilection for making the foolishness of one generation the wisdom of the next.

> *we must learn to think of the church humbly, as a workshop*

There was a play a number of years ago, entitled *The Sleeping Clergyman*. I did not see it, but having read about it, I am somehow unable to forget it. The curtain goes up with one character on stage: a clergyman, asleep in a chair. The curtain goes down. And then the curtain goes up on three of the most dramatic acts imaginable; and the curtain goes down. It comes up once again, and there is the clergyman, still sleeping. He has slept through the most dramatic and important events possible for a playwright to conceive. It is better, I would say, to make mistakes awake than to miss the show completely. It is better to seem to be foolish than to be irrelevant.

I would guess, and this is no casual guess but comes out of much thought and experience, that the future of this church will be chiefly dependent upon the degree of commitment which individual members have to ideals of service, and upon the willingness of individual members to face controversial issues. I would guess that the church makes its largest contribution to society by reminding its individual members that the kingdom of God is within, that their resources of courage and wisdom are limitless if they will but trust themselves. I would never minimize the role which the dedicated individual plays as a result of the inspiration he receives from the life of this church.

In the year 1900, on the occasion of the church's celebration of its 50th anniversary, one of its leading laymen, Horace Davis, said—and I think he said this with modesty—"I do not believe that any body of men and women in this state, of like size, yields a greater influence for good than does this church." I would venture, and I think not immodestly, to say the same thing in 1962. I doubt that there is a church in the San Francisco community of like size, with more of its membership seriously committed to social service and to idealistic objectives. Here in this area of the committed individual we will, in my judgment, continue to make our major thrust into the great life of society.

I am very proud, however, that we are experimenting in other directions. I am proud that our Social Action Committee and our Board of Trustees are directing our attention as a congregation to such issues as nuclear testing and shelters. I am proud that our Board of Trustees, at its last meeting, on the initiative of the Social Action Committee, petitioned Congress to pass proposed legislation which will make it possible for our government to purchase $100,000,000 worth of United Nations bonds. I am proud that the American Association for the United Nations will shortly hold a public meeting on this particular problem in our sanctuary. I am proud that our Board of Trustees at its last meeting, petitioned the Supervisors of our city to pass a Fair Housing Practices Ordinance which will make our city less a city of discrimination, as in fact it is today, and more a city of genuine brotherhood. I am proud that we are pioneering in a movement which might be called "Let the Congregation Speak," for the problems of the churches in America today is not that they are saying too much, but that they are saying too little on the matters that matter most.

It may well be, as actor Gary Merrill suggested earlier this morning, speaking in our sanctuary, that the major threat to our democracy is not the atomic nor the hydrogen bomb, but the feeling on the part of the great numbers of our citizens that somehow, in ways they do not understand, the fundamental processes of decision making have slipped out of their hands, so that they can do nothing but sit back and wait for their government to decide their fate; so that they are in danger of forgetting that we are the government, that this is what Lincoln's phrase means: "government of the people, by the people, for the people."

So I am saying to you this morning, let us speak as a congregation. Let us speak deliberately, carefully, not hastily, but honestly and earnestly to the issues of the day. Let us speak out of the awareness that our God is a God of love and justice, or he is not God. Let us speak not out of the feeling that our church is an infallible agency or that God speaks through no other agency, but let us speak because we know the church has a primary concern to shape the conscience of the nation. If its voice is not heard, then that conscience will be misshapen.

> *our God is a God of love and justice, or he is not God*

Let us speak knowing that we cannot speak without the torment of disagreement and even the possibility of division, but knowing that if our love and respect for truth are accompanied by a genuine humility and a growing affection for one another, even the divisions can be healed, and even deep disagreements can be brought within the spectrum of understanding. Let us speak lest the values which are at the heart of our faith become lost in a Babel of voices, lest religion becomes segregated out of the market place and the legislative halls, lest we forget the ancient truths that men do not live by bread alone but by every word that proceedeth from the mouth of the living God.

*****

NOTE

1. *The Churches and The Public*, published by the Center for the Study of Democratic Institutions, Santa Barbara, California, an activity of the Fund for the Republic. See Chapter II, "On meddling."

WITNESS FOR LIFE

[Address given by The Reverend Harry B. Scholefield, D.D., Minister of the First Unitarian Church of San Francisco, at the Civic Center Plaza, April 13, 1963]

As a minister, I often use texts to illustrate my thought. It is particularly appropriate that I do so this morning as we initiate our WITNESS FOR LIFE in this season of Passover and Easter. I have taken two texts, one from the Book of the Prophet Micah:

> Ye shall judge among many people, and rebuke strong nations afar off; and they shall beat their swords into ploughshares, and their spears into pruning hooks: nations shall not lift up a sword against nation, neither shall they learn war anymore.

and the other from the New Testament, words of Jesus of Nazareth taken from the Sermon on the Mount:

> *Blessed are the peacemakers: for they shall be called the children of God.*

We are concerned with the need to stop the senseless arms race and we are concerned to build the peace. Micah speaks of the God of Justice rebuking strong nations. We come together because we recognize there is dreadful peril in the continuation of an uncontrolled arms race, because we believe that the military policies of both the Soviet and American blocs constitute a menace to the peace of the world. We fear that the spending of billions upon billions of dollars on armaments in both our

We are concerned with the need to stop the senseless arms race

nation and the Soviet Union has carried us closer to the danger of war rather than farther away from it. We are asking ourselves what can be done to reverse the trend. We are terribly mindful of the judgment made by the noted British physicist, C.P. Snow, at the December 1960 meeting of the American Association for the Advancement of Science. He said, and he stressed the sense of responsibility with which he was speaking, he said that within ten years some of the nuclear weapons being manufactured and stored would go off. He pleaded with the scientists on the need for a negotiated agreement for the banning of nuclear weapons. Granted, he said, that there was a risk in any kind of agreement, the risk involved was less than the risks of continued testing. We are mindful of a statement made in a recent *New York Times* editorial (March 25, 1963) to the effect that within a decade there will not be four nuclear powers, there will be 15, 20 or 25. We gather here to express our conviction that both our government and that of the Soviet Union spare no effort to continue the negotiations until a test ban with adequate inspection is achieved.

Ours is an ancient concern. The concern with peace has long roots which go far back into the Judeo-Christian tradition and into the tradition of the other religions of the world. We gratefully acknowledge here a singular flowering of the concern for peace in the encyclical *Pacem in Terris* issued a few days ago (April 10, 1963) by His Holiness, Pope John XXIII. Personally, and as a Protestant minister in a liberal church, I am very moved by this encyclical. Let me refer you to certain of its passages:

> "...it is with deep sorrow that we note the enormous stocks of armaments that have been and still are being made in more economically developed countries, with a vast outlay of intellectual and economic resources. As so it happens that, while the people of these countries are loaded with heavy burdens, other countries as a result are deprived of the collaboration they need in order to make economic and social progress.

"The production of arms is allegedly justified on the grounds that in present-day conditions peace cannot by preserved without an equal balance of armaments. And so, if one country increases its armaments, others feel the need to do the same; and if one country is equipped with nuclear weapons, other countries must produce their own, equally destructive.

"Consequently, people live in constant fear lest the storm that every moment threatens should break upon them with dreadful violence. And with good reason, for the arms of war are ready at hand. Even though it is difficult to believe that anyone would deliberately take the responsibility for the appalling destruction and sorrow that war would bring in its train, it cannot be denied that the conflagration may be set off by some uncontrollable and unexpected chance. And one must bear in mind that, even though the monstrous power of modern weapons acts as a deterrent, it is to be feared that the mere continuance of nuclear tests, undertaken with war in mind, will have fatal consequences for life on earth.

> *people live in constant fear*

"Justice, then, right reason and humanity urgently demand that the arms race should cease. That the stockpiles which exist in various countries should be reduced equally and simultaneously by the parties concerned. That nuclear weapons should be banned. And that a general agreement should eventually be reached about progressive disarmament and an effective method of control. In the words of Pius XII, our predecessor of happy memory: 'The calamity of a world war, with the economic and social ruin and the moral excesses and dissolution that accompany it, must not be permitted to envelop the human race for a third time.' "

These words, addressed to all the nations of the world, fall with particular urgency upon ourselves and the Soviet Union and the other nuclear powers.

We gather here today also recognizing the tremendous importance of strengthening and supporting the United Nations. The serious fact today is that we continue to live as though our twentieth-century problems could be solved through the ancient method of reliance upon the power of the nation-state. Contemporary technological advance demands that we learn to think in terms of larger allegiances and visions than is now our habit and pattern. If we are unable to stop thinking merely in terms of the needs and interests of the nation-state, we shall think our way to mutual destruction. As American citizens who would also be world citizens, we must bring our thinking abreast of the times.

Strangely—or perhaps it is not so strange—no one is depicting our dilemma and our peril with more attentiveness and cogency than certain of our military leaders. General of the Army Douglas MacArthur described our plight well when he said, less than a year ago,

> The tremendous evolution of nuclear and other potentials of destruction has suddenly taken the problem [that is, the problem of war and peace] away from its primary consideration as a moral, and spiritual question, and brought it abreast of scientific realism. It is no longer an ethical equation to be pondered solely by learned philosophers and ecclesiastics, but a hard core one for the decision of the masses whose survival is the issue.... Many will tell you with mockery and ridicule that the abolition of war can only be a dream—that it is but the vague imagining of a visionary. But we must go on [toward this goal] or we will go under.

We are here this morning because we must go on with the goal of the abolition of war—because in these days of possible nuclear holocaust there is no realistic alternative to peace. We are here because we feel that peace with freedom and justice can only be achieved as greater numbers of individuals throughout the world earnestly commit themselves to it.

Blessed are the peacemakers: for they shall be called the children of God.

Ye shall judge among many people, and rebuke strong nations afar off; and they shall beat their swords into ploughshares, and their spears into pruning hooks: nation shall not lift up a sword against nation, neither shall they learn war anymore.

UNITARIANS ARE EGGHEADS

I am changing my sermon topic this morning from the question, ARE UNITARIANS EGGHEADS? to the simple declaratory statement, UNITARIANS ARE EGGHEADS, or UNITARIANS ASPIRE TO BE EGGHEADS.

What is an egghead? Webster's Third International Dictionary offers two definitions. The first is: "one with intellectual interests or pretensions." The second is: "a highly educated person."

Under the first definition we are given an illustrative sentence about a newspaper correspondent. The correspondent is not named, but the sentence reads, "He can be considered an egghead himself. (He boned up for covering the Korean war by reading Thucydides.)

We can offer a fairly practical definition, then, of the word—so far as it applies to newspaper correspondents—by saying that a newspaper correspondent is an egghead if, having been assigned to cover the Korean or the Vietnam war, he reads as preparation the works of the fourth century B. C. Greek historian Thucydides.

I suspect the word egghead originated in the thirties, during the great depression. President Roosevelt urged intellectuals to join him in Washington, D.C., to help the government fight the depression. President Roosevelt was a Harvard man himself, and partial to Harvard intellectuals. There used to be a saying then that when a man asked how to get to Washington, the answer was, "Go to Harvard Square and turn left." At any rate, one of the lessons that many learned during the depression was that brains were not necessarily a handicap to those who would serve their country. And today, except for political primitives—using the word primitive in a derogatory sense—professors, i.e., intellectuals, i.e., eggheads, are welcome in Washington, D.C., in Sacramento, and, apart from the capitals the Deep South, in almost every other capital in the land.

In its anatomical aspects, the word egghead probably derives from the popular assumption that persons with brains, large brains, invariably have high foreheads and receding hairlines, so that viewed from the front the long curved forehead resembles the smooth curved surface and shape of an egg.

Now what does this have to do with Unitarianism?—this is a frankly denominational type of sermon. From the time that Michael Servetus was burned at the stake in Geneva in 1553—Michael Servetus who said to the theologians of his day, "Your Trinity is the product of subtlety and madness, the Gospel knows nothing of it"—from that day to this Unitarians have sought to be distinguished not so much by any single doctrinal point as it was distinguished by an emphasis on reason in religion.

"Your Trinity is the product of subtlety and madness, the Gospel knows nothing of it"

The great scholar of Unitarianism, Earl Morse Wilbur, in his monumental work on Unitarianism in the sixteenth and seventeenth centuries, contended that the movement was distinguished not so much by any single doctrinal point as it was distinguished by three cardinal emphases in its churches.

1. An emphasis upon the use of reason in religion.

2. An emphasis upon the acceptance of diverse points of view in religion—what we call pluralism.

3. A parallel emphasis upon freedom of belief, that men have to shape their faiths freely out of their experience.

Skipping over two centuries and coming down to Unitarianism in its beginning phases in America, we find Thomas Jefferson saying, "I have sworn upon the altar of God eternal hostility to every form of tyranny over the mind of man." Jefferson believed in education more than in any formal religion. Indeed, he was deeply skeptical of Calvinistic churches, Catholic churches, because he felt they had men's minds in thralldom. He felt that the country was safe so long as men were taught to think, to use their minds freely and venturesomely in all areas of experience. He felt that democracy was lost—no matter how high its standard of living was, no matter how strong it looked from the outside—if its citizens did not now how to think for themselves.

Jefferson believed in education more than in any formal religion.

As a matter of fact, I think it could be argued that the Constitutional Convention which gathered in Philadelphia towards the end of the eighteenth century, and the men who were directly related to it: the Adamses, Jefferson, Franklin, Madison, Hamilton, and so forth, constituted one of the most remarkable gatherings of eggheads ever to come together under one roof. Our Constitution—and indeed our nation—is a remarkable testimony to the genius of their eggheadedness.

From Jefferson we go to William Ellery Channing, the foremost figure among the founders or inspirers of American Unitarianism, one of the trinity including Ralph Waldo Emerson and Theodore Parker. Channing said many things that bear witness to the egghead character of our tradition. One that I often recall is this sentence: "I am surer that my rational nature is from God than I am that any book is an expression of his will." In this sentence Channing showed that he had escaped from the kind of sterile eggheadedness that is unrelated to life. The stress here is from a book handed down from the past to man's rational nature exercised in the present. This is not to say that theory is unimportant, that practice is important. It is to say that theory is only important as it is related to the present, as it is related to living experience. Actually, Channing's statement is meaningful because it is ambiguous. It brings together both skepticism and belief: skepticism of past authorities, the books as being binding on the present; belief in the mind working in the present, belief that the truth will come out of experience if a road is cleared for it.

If eggheadism has at its center a nuclear aspiration to be rational, I believe there is no doubt that our tradition, extending back over four hundred years to Servetus, Socinus, Francis David, is heavily egghead.

What about the present?

One way to take our measure is to look at the people we travel with, our fellow-travelers who may not bear the Unitarian label but are very much at home with us, as we are at home with them.

I think you could take your life in your hands and give a fairly accurate picture of the main founts of contemporary inspiration for Unitarians as a whole; but to be safer, we should ask ourselves individually who the men and women are from whom we have gained stimulation and inspiration. Who are the ones on whom we are dependent, who are, in a deep sense, our friends?

If I were asked to name the six modern thinkers who have been most influential in my development as a person and in the formation of my intellectual frame of reference, I would name the following—and the order does not necessarily reflect priority:

SIGMUND FREUD, LEWIS MUMFORD, MARTIN BUBER, ERIK ERIKSON, ERICH FROMM, AND JULIAN HUXLEY.

If I were to name another half-dozen thinkers—thinkers who also act—some of whom I had difficulty keeping out of the first list, I would go on to name PAUL TILLICH, REINHOLD NIEBUHR, DAISETZ T. SUZUKI, LOREN EISLEY, HENRY NELSON WIEMAN, JOHN DEWEY, CARL JUNG. (Jung insisted on coming in just when I was shutting the gate behind John Dewey!)

Of course, I drew up my list very uneasily, fully aware that it may sound too grandiose, and fully aware that one cannot exclude the influence of teachers all the way from kindergarten to post-graduate study. Nor can one exclude the influence of poets, playwrights, painters and individuals who have touched one's life perhaps briefly but with tremendous and lasting impact. The point is that, for me, most of the people who are my luminaries would fit into the egghead constellation, the egghead category.

I should say, however, that there are different kinds of eggheadedness, and the kind I trust has certain marked characteristics. Let me list briefly four of them:

1. It is a humble eggheadedness. I often think of the remark—and since I am being chauvinistic, let me say it—the remark of the Unitarian, Mr. Justice Oliver Wendell Holmes. "The great act of faith comes," he said, "when man acknowledges that he is not God."

There is such a thing as a barren and sterile pride in intellect which assumes that intellect is the key that will unlock all mysteries. Sigmund Freud, of all people, is reported to have said, "In small matters trust the mind, but in the great matters, trust the heart."

"...in the great matters, trust the heart"

Our knowledge is a torch of smoking pine
That lights the darkness but one step ahead.

I like eggheadedness that never undersells the power of human knowledge but is perceptive enough and humble enough to know that men still, and, so far as we know, always will live by faith.

2. Eggheadism has never been the same since the advent of Sigmund Freud, for since Freud we know explicitly the nature of the phenomenon called rationalization. We say a thing is true not because it is true but because we want it to be true. Eggheadism which deals with conscious thought as though it were unrelated to unconscious motivation is really like a bird trying to fly with one wing. This has been, and may still be, a weakness of much Unitarian eggheadism,

that it can be like one of those hydrofoil boats in which tourists take short trips on the Seine River in Paris or the Neva River in Leningrad: they skim the surface with tremendous speed and ease, but do not plumb the depths. In very rough storms on the open seas, I presume they would be a bit like the corks of champagne bottles which are sometimes used as playthings for kittens. I want an eggheadism that hangs fast and doggedly, amidst all circumstances, to this faith in the human mind—but doesn't forget that the mind is human.

3. I want an eggheadism that does not take refuge in abstractions. Large abstractions about the nature of man: his goodness or badness, his mechanical nature or animal heart, his naturalism or supernaturalism, are the modern version of the Scholastic's question, "How many angels can dance on the head of a pin?"

I suppose, when Gertrude Stein is reputed to have said *a rose is a rose is a rose*, this was one of the things we all get at: a rose is a combination of chemical compounds, a unit of solar energy, an economic unit that brings so much in a florist's shop—but it is also a rose. It has fragrance, and it is very beautiful, particularly in its relationship to the weatherbeaten trellis on the back doorstep. A man is also a combination of chemicals, which years ago was valued at about $2.39 and could be held in a small jar or box, the kind that comes from the crematory. But he is also something else. He is Tom Jones, or Ronald Smith, or Harry Scholefield.

4. I indicated at the beginning of the sermon that *Webster's Third International Dictionary* illustrated the meaning of the word egghead with a sentence about a reporter who "boned up for covering the Korean war by reading Thucydides."

There is a remarkable article in the current (September) issue of *Harper's* Magazine telling the story of the destruction of an American platoon in a battle which took place last May in the central highlands of Vietnam. A *Look* Magazine correspondent, Sam Castan, was with the platoon. He was there, as he said to the division's Public Information Officer, because "I wish to know the thoughts of men facing death." The Public Information Officer questioned whether Castan's death was logical, "men's fears and reflections not being all of one kind, and the soldier hardly knowing how he thinks of death until he feels he is dying."

Castan was on the battle site eagerly questioning Sergeant Edward Shepherd when the first shots were fired, and the sergeant died right in front of him. When the American unit of 22 men was driven off the hill, practically decimated, Castan was wounded—he had taken a bullet in one arm and grenade fragments in his back. He had the courage of a lion, and decided that he would run for such safety as he could find. He moved in long strides straight to the trail which led downhill through elephant grass.

"Standing clear on the trail was an enemy soldier, rifle aimed. The exemplary leader of the platoon, a man of tremendous bravery and presence of mind, Sergeant Robert L. Kirby, a 29-year-old Negro from Los Angeles, heard a scream as Castan went down." Though Castan was not fifteen yards from him, Kirby could not see the fall, as the body was enveloped by the sea of grass. But he heard the thump of the body. The bullet had drilled the magazine correspondent through his left temple.

"Castan's personal effects were looted soon after he fell. But his camera and his purse were later recovered from the bodies of enemy dead in a fight that soon followed." From the films in the recovered camera were developed the pictures—part of the *Harper* article-taken by Castan just before the platoon was destroyed.

I don't know whether Castan read Thucydides as preparation for going to Vietnam. I know nothing about him except that he was an unusual man with his questions about the way men face death in battle, and his bravery.

But he tells me that the only kind of eggheadism that is worthwhile is the eggheadism that is where the action is—it might be Hereford Hill in the central highlands of Vietnam, it might be a pacifist battleground like Port Chicago. Deep eggheadism leads to commitment and action. All other kinds of eggheadism are phony, or at least ineffective.

WHAT I HEAR MYSELF SAYING

Bishop A.T. Robinson, in his highly personal little theological tract called *Honest to God*, is so concerned with the misuses of the word "God" that he finds himself sympathetic with the suggestion that the word should be dropped from our language for the space of a generation. This would give us time to rid it of the confused usages which have made it a basketful of irrelevancies. The suggestion reminds me of another suggestion made ten or fifteen years ago, a more modest one. It was suggested that all ministers should stop preaching for one year. Those supporting this moratorium felt that preaching has become largely irrelevant. Whether it's irrelevant or relevant, they have a serious question in their mind as to whether anyone is listening.

> *It was suggested that all ministers should stop preaching for one year*

I think of a moratorium on preaching because I am about to have one. This morning's sermon will be my last for nine Sundays—barring unforeseen contingencies. I sometimes think that only a person who has been in the pulpit over a long period of time—say twenty or twenty-five years—can appreciate the difficulties and gratifications, the honesties and dishonesties, the exposure and concealments, the failures and the triumphs which the craft demands. I am moving into my twenty-fifth year of continuous occupancy of the pulpit. The pulpits I have occupied within that time have varied enormously, from this historic Starr King pulpit to pulpits on trains, on shipboard, in hospitals and prisons, in mess-halls and in all the varied places that the parish ministry and the overseas military chaplaincy takes a preacher.

The mechanics of preaching are simple enough—simple, but tyrannical and constant. In our church the preacher must give his sermon title to the church by Tuesday, 10:00 am. The sermon topic must be accompanied by an explanatory paragraph or two with respect to its projected contents. The sad, recurring fact is that Tuesday always follows Sunday. I sometimes think on Tuesday of that remark of Hamlet's to the effect that the funeral meats are used to serve the wedding guests. He is referring sardonically to the fact that the marriage of his uncle to his mother followed hard upon the funeral of his father, murdered at the hand of his uncle. This is a grim analogy. I used it to illustrate the fact that the echoes of one Sunday sermon have scarcely been erased from the tape recorder before the mouth of the typewriter gapes for the title of the next homiletic offering.

Once in a sermon I compared the preacher to the Greek hero, Sisyphus, who was condemned by the gods to roll a great stone to the top of a high mountain, whence the stone perpetually rolls back of its own dead weight. The gods thought, and rightly so, as Albert Camus puts it, that there is no more dreadful punishment to be visited upon man than unceasingly futile and hopeless labor. Applying this analogy to preaching, we can say that the sermon is a rock. Every week the minister rolls it up the long hill of preparation. He lets go of it at approximately 11:30 a.m. every Sunday. It rolls back. He descends from the pulpit and then proceeds down the long path to the bottom of the Monday hill to begin rolling it up again.

You may say that this analogy does not hold with exactitude because though the sermon may roll off the backs of those who hear it on Sunday, and off the back of the man who gives it, it is always a different rock. The preacher has at least this advantage over Sisyphus. Every week he rolls up a different stone. But this objection will not hold. If you had listened to all the sermons I have delivered from this pulpit during the past year, or, perish the mark, during the past six years since you called me to this pulpit, you would have undoubtedly sensed that although there were many different sermons, they were built basically around a few themes. Near the house in which I loved as a boy, there was a large exposure of rock which had on it in clear and unmistakable fashion the marking of a glacier which had moved across it, millions of years earlier. There it stood and there it stands, testifying to glacial directions. We all have a kind of basic marking upon what we do and what we say. If markings have been running north to south they are not likely to change suddenly and run from east to west. Even if they do change in content, there will be a basic continuing sameness about our posture and about our motion. Our stance has become us. We cannot throw it off.

We all have a kind of basic marking upon what we do and what we say

Let me ask myself—although the question might be better addressed to you—what have I said, or what have I been trying to say in the past year's sermons? What are the repetitive concerns that run through them? What are the deeper fears and hopes and glacial markings?

I hear myself constantly being impatient with theology, and yet drawn increasingly to the quest for meaning. I am constantly buffeted between frustration at the fact that patterns of meaning shift, and longing to find a constant pattern against which I can brace myself, in which I can take permanent satisfaction.

How often our feelings and intellects go in opposite directions.

How often what we have thought was a lasting answer to life's eternal mysteries turns out to be transient and ephemeral. We think we have the key which opens all the doors and then we find that someone has changed the locks on us. It is like a dream in the midst of which we come easily and happily to the realization that we have discovered the key to the mystery of existence, but alas, we cannot recall the dream!

Why not throw out the theology? Why not dispense with the quest for meaning at the level of rationality and settle simply for our feelings? Why not latch onto complete subjectivity and be swallowed up by the feelings we wallow in? The answer is in the nature of our needs. The need for rational comprehension is simply there—like a mountain, a river or a star, like the morning star, like the morning mist, the sunset, like light and darkness. I listen to what I am saying in my sermons and suddenly I see that I am a swinger. I am very grateful to Sidney Cox for his small book on Robert Frost in which he characterized Frost as a "swinging poet." I feel a bit easier in my own swinging role when I reflect that Robert Frost is one who has broken the path for me.

> *When I see birches bend to left and right*
> *Across the lines of straighter, darker trees,*
> *I like to think some boy's been swinging them*
> *But swinging doesn't bend them down to stay...*
> *I'd like to get away from earth awhile*
> *And then come back to it and begin over...*
> *I'd like to go by climbing a birch tree,*
> *And climb black branches up a snow white trunk*
> *Toward heaven, till the tree could bear no more,*
> *But dip its top and set me down again.*
> *That would be good both going and coming back,*
> *One could do worse than be a swinger of birches.*

I see in my sermons that I swing between the need to recognize that answers are important and the need to recognize that there is no answer which will not burst as we grow into a larger life together. I swing between the need to recognize that all answers are ephemeral and the need to find "hints of eternity in the images of time." I swing between the need to find a formula for personal growth and social change and the need to recognize that personal growth and social change are vital processes which cannot be confined to any single intellectual formula. "A swinging approach" is an apt phrase to describe what I hear myself saying.

Another theme which recurs throughout my sermons is a continual concern with the riddle of *human choice*, the fact of decision. Do we make choices? Or are our choices and decisions always predetermined, predestined? Here is the clash between determinism and free will which in every generation puts on a different costume and struts across the stage. If I look at this question theoretically, it becomes a head-spinning question. Facing it, I am reminded of those moments when I tried to follow a jet plane in the clear sky. I have the jet in focus, but despite intense concentration, it slips imperceptibly beyond my field of vision. It does this at the very moment I think that its speeding form will not elude me.

are our choices and decisions always predetermined, predestined?

I hear myself saying again and again in my sermons that life is an uncertain business. We have no control over large and vital areas of our experience. In these areas where we don't control the events which overtake us, life's sad accidents, the reality of fate, as portrayed in the Greek tragedies, is beyond dispute. Life says to us what it said to Walt Whitman.

> *Listen! I will be honest with you;*
> *I do not offer the old smooth prizes,*
> *but offer rough new prizes;*
> *These are the days that must happen to you ....*

If in the face of the "fate" which overtakes me I raise questions as to meaning—and of course I do—seeking some intellectual solution, the answers which come back are all paradoxical. A contemporary theologian seeking to bring back freedom and determinism together in some sensible formula makes the comment, "freedom is a growing awareness of determinism." He leads us here into a paradox. We have the feeling that we are dealing now with opposites that cannot be reconciled.

I have no coherent theoretical answer. Practically, however, I must have an answer. I hear myself stating an article of faith which is stubbornly persistent. I believe that we are "fated" in certain areas of experience, areas of grave significance. But I believe that in all areas we have a measure of freedom to determine the nature of our response to fate. I like the analogy which comes out of the wisdom of India, to the effect that *life must be thought of as a card game*. The fates determine the hand which is dealt to us, but we are free to play the hand as we will. We have the freedom to manifest wisdom and courage. We have the freedom to manifest the power of patience and the power of impatience. We make the choices between character and non-character. We choose what kind of person we will become, what we will make of the existence which has been lent to us. We determine whether we will be hating, loving, productive, non-productive, altruistic, selfish. We can widen our horizons. We can live in dark rooms with shut windows. We can commit ourselves to war and self-destruction. I hear myself saying often that the problem at most levels of life—in the realm of social challenge and in the realm of private growth—is not that we make the *wrong* choices, but that we make no choices, unless drifting on the seas of apathy be also a choice. We choose not to choose. As I listen to my sermons, it becomes clear that a most important article in my credo is that choice is in our hands. We can make the choice to live or we can make the choice to die. I hear myself saying that the man who makes wrong choices is more alive, more in relationship to Being, than the man who makes no choice.

Here is still another theme I hear myself discussing again and again. I am asking myself continually if there is more to human life than human beings making choices? Is there more to human existence than human existence?

Late one night several years ago I sat in a hotel room talking with a friend of mine who is a psychoanalyst. We were attending a conference together. He is a rationalist, or an agnostic. He may be an atheist in the positive and productive sense of the word. I am not sure. Labels are very slippery. I had been meditating for some weeks in my period of daily meditation on certain lines of the mystic Hindu poet, Rabindranath Tagore. They are saturated, as all of Tagore's poetry is, with a mystic sense of an all-encompassing Being. They spoke to my condition. I brought them into my conversation with the psychoanalyst and requested his reaction to them. They are, of course, a prayer-poem.

> *I ask for a moment's indulgence to sit by Thy side.*
> *The works that I have in hand I will finish afterwards.*
> *Away from the sight of Thy face my heart knows no rest or respite,*
> *And my work becomes an endless toil in a shoreless sea.*
> *Today summer has come at my window with its sighs and its murmurs;*
> *And the bees are plying their minstrelsy at the court of the flowering grove.*
> *Now it is time to sit quiet, face to face with Thee, and to*
> *sing dedication of life in this silent and overflowing leisure.*

"What comes to your mind," I said, "does any bell ring?" "Of course," he said, "they are lovely lines. What comes to my mind is the recollection of sitting with some person I love and entering more deeply into life because of that love." "Does anything more come to mind?" I persisted. "No," he said quietly, "isn't that enough?"

I thought I would try him further. I quoted some lines from a Greek source, an epitaph written by sailors shipwrecked on a lonely coast.

> *Some shipwrecked sailors buried on this coast*
> *Bid you set sail.*

Full many a gallant bark when we were lost
Weathered the gale.

Immediately he spoke enthusiastically of these lines and requested a copy of them. It was not that they said more than the lines from Tagore, they simply said more to him.

There is no hint in them—or is there a hint?—of a tide coming in from beyond the human spectrum to salvage the broken event, to redeem the irretrievable loss. There is in them a clean and sparkling sense of the joy that others succeeded where the shipwrecked sailors went down. There is in these lines the assumption that for our human venture, nothing is more basic than the faith we cherish in one another—the faith that when we go down, others go on.

In my sermons I hear ambivalence on this point. I travel back and forth swinging again—or still—between a mystical poet like Tagore and my rational, twentieth-century, scientifically oriented, psychoanalytic friend. I travel back and forth between the part of me which says there is a goodness in all life which is transcendent, a hound of heaven, that which pursues me, and another part of me which says that there is nothing on earth but human effort. There is man only. We pin our dreams on the earth's surface. Life is gossamer. It is pertinent, by the way, to reflect on the derivation of "gossamer." Here is a word to conjure with. It is derived from the expression, "goose-summer" which refers to a period of mild weather in November when the geese were eaten. Life is gossamer. We perform our little works which last for seconds in a chain of aeons. There is nothing to life except transiency. Life is a brief period of mild weather in which we eat geese.

Life is a brief period of mild weather in which we eat geese

I see myself pitching my tent a bit closer to Tagore than to my psychoanalyst friend. But I confess my ambivalence. I hear myself saying—and this testifies to the reconciling impulse which is strong in me—that my friend the psychoanalyst and the poet Tagore are closer together than we think. Perhaps our problem is that we are too inclined to think of truth as straight lines which must run parallel without ever meeting. But can truth also be symbolized in two lines that cross one another? In curved lines or in circles? In thoughts which are contradictory?

This is what I hear myself asking. Now we go back to Sisyphus, where I started. I compared the task of the preacher to Sisyphus rolling the rock up the hill and seeing it roll down again endlessly. That sounds gloomy. Is preaching such an exercise in complete frustration? Is it always labor that is futile and hopeless? No. I have given you a description which is too one-sided. All sermons do not roll off the backs of those who hear them, or of those who give them. There is satisfaction in the enterprise as well as the frustration. There is happiness as well as despair. The words with which Camus concludes his essay on Sisyphus are apropos:

> "I leave Sisyphus at the foot of the mountain! One always finds one's burden again. But Sisyphus teaches the higher fidelity that negates the gods and raises rocks. He too concludes that all is well. The universe, henceforth without a master, seems to him neither sterile nor futile. Each atom of that stone, each mineral flake of that night-filled mountain, in itself forms a world. The struggle itself toward the heights is not enough to fill a man's heart. One must imagine Sisyphus happy."

PRAYERS THAT STICK TO MY RIBS

Probably the most important thing about a prayer for me is that it should be useful. I keep an anthology of "useful" prayers. They are extremely varied. They come from all ages and from different aspects of the human condition: from moods of frustration and desperation to moods of thanksgiving and celebration. They delight me by their beauty and aptness, by their diversity and their particularity. They frustrate me sometimes by their theological assumptions and language. But the most important thing is that in one way or another they are useful to me.

This morning I am not getting into my theological frustrations. I'll try to be as pragmatic as possible and as personal as necessary.

Pragmatism is very much a part of our tradition. It has been said that Jews pray to the Father God, Catholics to Mary the Mother of God, Christian Scientists to the Mother-Father God, and Unitarian Universalists to "Whom it May Concern." This is practicality and pragmatism. Such a broad approach makes it possible to offer prayers to anything under the sun or, for that matter, above the sun. I find that breadth of conception useful.

THAT-TO-WHICH prayers are addressed has many shapes and forms. In our Judeo-Christian way of thinking it has become, over the centuries, too narrowly male—white male.

In very ancient cultures—predating the Old Testament—on clay tablets and on papyrus, prayers are addressed to gods and goddesses without discrimination. It may have been the Babylonian Job who said unhappily:

I prayed to my God and he did not listen;
I prayed to my Goddess and she did not even lift her head.

Conventional prayers are apt to be too chauvinistically male in their language, and too exclusively monotheistic. Polytheism is alive, however, among the poets.

To Walt Whitman, for example, the whole universe was alive, as so he speaks to the road on which his is walking:

You road I enter upon and look around, I believe you are not all that is here,
I believe that much unseen is also here.

and he goes on to speak to other surrounding presences:

You air that serves me with breath to speak!
You objects that call from diffusion my meanings and give them shape!
You light that wraps me and all things in delicate equable showers!
You paths worn in the irregular hollows by the roadsides!
I believe you are latent with unseen existences, you are so dear to me.

This dialogue with "unseen existences" in the things around us is akin to prayer.

Another example, the great Chilean poet, Pablo Neruda, holds a prayer-dialogue with the salt in a salt shaker:

Dust of the sea, the tongue
receives a kiss
of the night sea from you:
taste recognizes
the ocean in each salted morsel,
And therefore the smallest,
the tiniest

wave of the shaker
brings home to us
not only your domestic whiteness
but the inward flavor of the infinite.

Prayer is a form of conversation with mystery. I experience it as conversation with the multiple, mysterious facets and realities of the living universe.

Not only do the realities to which prayer is addressed vary enormously, but the same is true of the uses to which prayer is put—even among Christians.

One of my favorite prayer-stories is a story about a lion hunter. This lion hunter spotted a lion at the precise moment he was spotted by the lion. Simultaneously the lion charged and he raised his gun to his shoulder and fired. Unfortunately his gun jammed. He knew he was lost. Nothing to do but to fall to his knees and close his eyes in prayer. Nothing happened. He opened his eyes a crack and saw that the lion was kneeling in prayer beside him. "Oh," he said, "then you're a Christian too." To which the lion replied, "Of course." Then he looked at the man quizzically and said, "I don't know what you're praying about, but I am saying grace!"

The cynic listens to this story and thinks it just proves how confused and meaningless prayer is. I listen to it and think that it just proves how human it is to pray for help in a dire emergency.

It's human, but is it helpful? There are a lot of people who would argue that these prayers of desperation are not answered. I don't know about that, but I do know that they are a very human reaction to impossible stress and danger. And I also know that people who would be embarrassed to admit it resort to them in direst need!

I use prayers primarily to clarify my intentions, strengthen my will and shape my attitudes towards others and towards life. So my prayers are part of my daily living and thinking. They are helpful in times of crisis, but that is not a primary aim for cultivating them.

I think it is wise and practical that organizations like Alcoholics Anonymous and Narcotics Anonymous include the Serenity Prayer in their public rituals and urge its regular use in private:

God, give me the serenity to accept what can't be changed,
the courage to change what can be changed,

and the wisdom to know the difference.

Just what the word "God" may mean in that prayer is left to the individual to determine. I am impressed with the fact that here are people with very serious problems on their hands who, through this prayer, are regularly and intentionally trying to live with serenity, courage and wisdom.

The very act of establishing such goals as these, and a regular constant focus on them, can make tremendous differences in the way we live. I certainly have proved this to myself in my own life and I use many prayers to this end.

For example, this line from a prayer by the late Peter Marshall, slightly adapted:

God, help me to stand for something lest I fall for nothing.

helps keep me from being too indecisive, not to say wishy-washy!

Or this one, also from Peter Marshall, is a good antidote to presumptuousness, not to say arrogance:

God, when we have the truth, help us not to hit each other
over the head with it, but, rather, use it as a lamp to lighten
the dark places.

It was a bit over fifty years ago that I was a student at the Harvard Divinity School. I still have a copy of the little book of Morning Prayers printed for use at the daily services in the chapel of the University Memorial Church. And some of those prayers have stuck to my ribs for over half a century and have been immensely useful.

For example, this one which I have occasionally used here at our Sunday morning services. I'm sure that some of you will recognize it. It has helped to keep me steady.

Fix thou our steps, O Lord, that we stagger not at the uneven motions of the world, but go steadily on our way, neither censuring our journey by the weather we meet, nor turning aside for anything that befalls us.

Or this one: I'm not sure I can read it without my voice breaking. It has a high emotional voltage for me right now. I've asked my son, Joel, who is our Unitarian Universalist Minister in Marin to stand by if I need help.

God of all our life, help us when the task seems hard, when the road seems long, when the skies are grey with clouds which return after the rain, and when there is no song in our hearts. Then show us the easy yoke, set our feet with new patience in the way of life, quicken our ears to hear the morning stars singing together, and teach us that thou art where the shadows fall.

Well, I did get through it, but it does indeed have a high emotional voltage for me!

I said at the outset that the range of prayers I find useful is wide and inclusive. For example, there is this line from Sappho's prayer to Aphrodite:

Save me from the sorrow that grows too bitter.

or these words at the beginning of a prayer in Aeschylus' Agamemnon:

O Zeus, our God and our darkness, Giver of beauty and power,

The concept of God as darkness is a powerful one for me.

I love prayers that have stood the test of not merely fifty years but of millennia. For example, this prayer at the end of Plato's dialogue, the Phaedrus, offered by Socrates:

Beloved Pan and all ye other gods who haunt this place, give me beauty in the inward soul; and may the outward and inward man be at one. May I reckon the wise to be the wealthy, and may I have only as much gold as a temperate person can carry.

This morning Alex Post has played several pieces of great organ music inspired by the Lord's Prayer. I don't use the Lord's Prayer much, though I respect the power it has for those who do use it. A recollection comes back to me. I remember that during the Second World War when, as an army chaplain, I was stationed in bombed-out cities, I occasionally stood before huge mounds of rubble and repeated the Lord's Prayer silently or aloud. I don't know why I did this. It was as though I was trying to find some meaning *in* or bring some meaning *to* places of utter desolation.

Among the most meaningful prayers for me are prayers of thanksgiving that rise out of doubt and suffering. That is why I read earlier the poem *Human Being* by Denise Levertov. It says so much of what I have tried to say this morning that I'll use it as my closing words:

Human being—walking
in doubt from childhood on: walking
a ledge of slippery stone in the world's woods
deep-layered with wet leaves—rich or sad: on one
side of the path, ecstacy, on the other
dull grief   Walking
the mind's imperial cities, roofed-over alleys.
                         thoroughfares,
                         wide boulevards
that hold evening primrose of sky in steady calipers.
Always the mind,

*walking, working, stopping sometimes to kneel
in awe of beauty, sometimes leaping, filled with energy
of delight, but never able to pass
the wall, the wall
of brick that crumbles and is replaced,
of twisted iron,
of rock,
the wall that speaks, saying monotonously:*
     *Children and animals
      who cannot learn
   anything from suffering,
   suffer, are tortured, die
   in incomprehension.*
This human being, each night nevertheless
summoning—with a breath blown at a flame,
      or hand's touch
on the lamp-switch—darkness
      silently utters,
impelled as if by a need to cup the palms
and drink from a river,
      the words, "Thanks.
Thanks for this day, a day of my life."
      And wonders.
Pulls up the blankets, looking
into nowhere, always in doubt.
And takes strange pleasure
in having repeated once more the childish formula,
a pleasure in what is seemly.
And drifts to sleep, downstream
on murmuring currents of doubt and praise,
the wall shadowy, that tomorrow
will cast its own familiar, chill, clear-cut shadow
into today's brilliance.

THINK, THANK, ACT!

[RESPONSE MADE BY HARRY B. SCHOLEFIELD, MINISTER EMERITUS OF THE FIRST UNITARIAN CHURCH OF SAN FRANCISCO, ON RECEIVING THE ANNUAL AWARD FOR DISTINGUISHED SERVICE TO THE CAUSE OF UNITARIAN UNIVERSALISM PRESENTED BY THE UNITARIAN UNIVERSALIST ASSOCIATION AT ITS GENERAL ASSEMBLY HELD IN MILWAUKEE, WISCONSIN, JUNE 24, 1990.]

In accepting this award, I recognize that my ministry has been much more a community enterprise than an individual achievement. It has been drastically affected by events largely beyond my control and shaped by a host of different persons.

Foremost among those persons was Sarah, to whom I was married for nearly forty-seven years. She died in October of 1986. We did ministry together. Because I was ordained and male, I got most of the recognition. There were some exceptions. When we taught jointly at Meadville, her presence was a ministry, and was so recognized by both students and faculty. Then, there was the occasion when David Rankin left the San Francisco Church for Atlanta. It was typical of David that he invited both Sarah and me to participate in his Installation, Sarah to give the Charge to the Congregation, I to give the sermon. After the service, a woman came to me, looked me straight in the eye and said, "You were good, but Sarah was terrific!"

I'm willing to let that judgement stand.

As I have thought both of Sarah and of this occasion, I have been haunted a bit by the memory of Virginia Wolfe's essay, "A Room of One's Own". It has occurred to me that if Sarah had been ordained,

I might have been sitting out there with you on an occasion such as this, and she might have been up here.

Also, the persons who have been influential in shaping my life and career are my three children, five grandchildren, and a nine months old step-great grandchild who is a potent educative force at the present time.

Those of us who are ordained ministers are ministered to in so many ways by individuals in our congregations. Here is a small example. Once, in a sermon, I quoted Emerson's observation that everything God made has a crack in it. After the sermon, a young man came to me. He was greatly excited. He said, "Harry, do you know why God put the cracks in everything?" And before I had a chance to confess my ignorance, he answered his own question, "So that we can see through the disasters of the present time the better world we are building today for tomorrow."

Emerson's observation that everything God made has a crack in it

Ministry is mutual. I have often experienced a wonderful, healing irony. I have been inspired by the courage and wisdom of those who have sought my help. All the time that they were giving me credit for helping them, they were inspiring me!

This applies to whole congregations as well as to individuals. For ten years, I was minister of the First Unitarian Church of Philadelphia. While there, I had an unusual opportunity to do graduate study at the Philadelphia Psychoanalytic Institute. This required a comprehensive study of psychoanalytic literature, particularly the writings of Freud. It also required that I undergo psychoanalysis. I eventually graduated from the institute. It was a big project. The Philadelphia congregation respected both my desire and my need to undertake it. They shared my perception that the best foundation for outreach is inreach. They knew that self-knowledge is especially important in ministry. They knew that introspection and action are not separate realities, but two sides of the same coin. They made the project possible.

Through the nineteen-sixties, I had the privilege of being the senior minister of our San Francisco Church. I have always been grateful that in those turbulent years the San Francisco congregation had its priorities for ministry in good order. (I think Victor Carpenter would agree that it still does.)

Tip O'Neill used to say that the first rule in politics is to carry your own precinct. The San Francisco congregation expected me to carry my own precinct, that is, to be pre-eminently a parish minister always concerned with and involved in the joys and sorrows of its members. They recognized that we all live as individuals in a windy, wild and wonderful universe and that in our individual lives "everything tied down is always coming loose." But they also expected me to be a citizen minister playing an active role in civic affairs and humanitarian causes. The congregation did not merely condone, it challenged its ministers to be active in the civil rights struggles of the sixties, and in the anti-Vietnam war peace movement. Such activities were not always comfortable. There were disagreements among us leading at times to acrimony and even bitterness. But they were the signs of the times and a necessary part of living in the times.

to be a citizen minister playing an active role in civic affairs and humanitarian causes

San Francisco, and Philadelphia too, wanted its ministry to extend to the denomination. They understood that the local church is part of a larger movement which it sustains and by which it is sustained. In difficult times especially—I think of the McCarthy era in Philadelphia—they knew the truth of Benjamin Franklin's statement, which I paraphrase slightly, that either we hang together in a strong continental association, or we'll be hanged separately.

In recent years, mine has been a teaching ministry. I have taught at Meadville and Starr King, and led seminars and workshops across the continent at minister's institutes, districts churches and fellowships. My theme has been "The Singing River—The Daily Use of Poetry and Bibles." My concerns have been twofold. First, that we cultivate ways of making our great human heritage of poetry and bibles part of our daily living. This heritage is constantly being created and recreated and we can be part of the process. My second concern is that we become more aware of the central importance of the inner life, and that we cultivate regular private devotional practices. As might be expected, I find that our devotional practices are infinitely varied. There is much going on, and it's a rich mix. The concern for these matters is widespread, and that augurs well for our future.

Sometimes it seems to me that what we are all about as Unitarian Universalists can be summed up in just three words. The first word is ACT. Don't just stand there. ACT.

The other two words come to me through a Quaker friend. She went one Sabbath day to an old New Jersey meeting house. It turned out to be what the Quakers call a "gathered meeting," a meeting where no one speaks and the silence grows deeper and deeper. Fifteen minutes, a half hour, three quarters of an hour went by and nothing was said. The only sound in the meeting house was the ticking of an old grandfather's clock. As the meeting was about to close, a woman rose and said, "I've been sitting here trying to understand what the clock is saying to us. Now I think I've got it. It's saying, 'Think. Thank.' 'Think. Thank.' 'Think. Thank.'

I feel that I'm an old grandfather's clock that has been ticking away in our ministry for fifty-two years. And what I hear myself saying to you now in celebration of this occasion is,

Think. Thank. Act!

Think. Thank. Act!

Think. Thank. Act!

PSYCHOANALYSIS AND THE PARISH MINISTRY

[AN ADDRESS DELIVERED AT THE 142ND ANNUAL MEETING OF THE BERRY STREET CONFERENCE, MAY 23, 1962, IN WASHINGTON, D.C.]

In the course of a ten-year pastorate in Philadelphia, I had the opportunity to undertake an educative analysis under the auspices of the Philadelphia Psychoanalytic Institute. I began the didactic work and a personal analysis in the spring of 1954, and was graduated from the Institute in the spring of 1959. The core of the educative analysis program of the Institute is the personal analysis. In addition, the candidate for graduation must fulfill certain academic requirements, such as seminars, lecture courses, and extensive reading in the field of psychoanalysis, particularly the works of Freud. There are written examinations, and finally a paper and an oral examination, which, with the other requirements, determine the candidate's readiness for graduation.

In this paper I shall consider some of the aspects of the educative analysis as they relate to the parish ministry. First, I wish to discuss the relation of the educative analysis to my preaching. Then I shall offer some general and speculative observations about pastoral counseling, speculations deriving in part from the educative analysis, in part from my own involvement in the counseling process, and in part from my reading and study of the subject.

The effect of analysis upon my preaching

To say that the sermon composition has always been difficult for me is an understatement. It has always aroused anxieties that, I suspected, were far beyond any normal professional hazards. It was inevitable that many hours in my psychoanalysis would focus upon the problems of preaching, particularly that of sermon preparation. Through the weeks and months and years of my participation in the analytic process, some of the unconscious meanings related to the preaching process, as I experienced it, became apparent.

I gradually became aware specifically of factors that previously I had recognized only in a general sense as causes of anxiety. I became conscious of ways in which I was using my sermons for purposes I had not recognized before. I remember very well the analytic hour when I meant to say "sermon composition" and, tripped up by my unconscious, said "sermon competition."

Let me now list some of my discoveries, or "uncoveries."

I became aware of ways in which I was using my sermons to conceal myself from my congregation, rather than to share myself. I began to say ironically that a sermon is the minister's means of concealing his deeper feelings and concerns from his congregation.

I noted the subtle ways—and some not so subtle—in which, in my sermons, I would use the "solid" quotation, the experience of others, the eminent authority, not really as a means of exposition or elucidation, but actually as a means of putting someone between myself and the listening congregation.

I came to understand the meaning of "displacement," and began to see how I had displaced upon patterns of sermon preparation fears and anxieties originating in experiences of early life and in my earliest relationships. I had, of course, studied "displacement" in the psychoanalytic literature and was familiar with it as a device or mechanism; but it became an elemental fact that I had to learn about myself, and it had many meanings with reference to my pulpit work.

I became aware of elements of basic distrust of life and a kind of sterile skepticism that interfered greatly with sermon preparation and that I had previously rationalized as intellectual doubt.

Wrestling with the problems of expression of belief, I realized that doubt can be as compulsively neurotic as can faith.

I became conscious of a fear of emptiness and impoverishment in sermon preparation that was not a realistic fear, but a neurotic anxiety. I came to call it the "fear-of-the-empty-cupboard-complex"—the fear, that is, that when I went to prepare a sermon there would be nothing in the cupboard either for my own or for the congregation's nourishment. This can be more properly described as neurotic anxiety than as fear, for it was a substantial block to sermon preparation, even when my mind was well-stoked with ideas and my days well-filled with vital and growing experiences.

I became aware that I cherished much unconscious resentment against the sermon form, as well as against the form of the liturgy and the order of worship. This unconscious resentment stood in the way of my full utilization of these forms.

This unconscious resentment stood in the way of my full utilization of these forms.

I recognized the fact that I was sensitive to criticism to an exaggerated degree, and that I was unable to express mildly aggressive feelings without an unrealistic fear of retaliation on the congregation's part.

My need to be right, I learned, existed in highly exaggerated dimensions.

I became increasingly aware of my tendency to think of the sermons as "make work," a kind of ecclesiastical feather-bedding. It was, indeed, fortunate for me that my congregation almost invariably placed a much higher evaluation on my sermon work than I did. But it is also significant that the fact that they did so created additional problems for me because of my lack of self-acceptance. The inability to accept and genuinely and honestly to enjoy a compliment indicates a lack of self-acceptance.

I became aware of ways in which my ability to communicate ideas and feelings was quite literally fouled up by my inner conflicts, so that, for example, I unconsciously expressed hostility when I meant to speak love and understanding.

No discipline places more emphasis upon the potentially curative effects of knowledge of the past than does psychoanalysis. Hence I must now say a word about my personal history.

At the age of five, under tragic circumstances, I lost both my father and my mother. My father disappeared. My mother committed suicide. My three brothers—two younger and one older—and I were placed in an orphanage. The youngest brother died shortly of diphtheria. The next youngest, only a year younger than I, drowned when I was ten. This left an older brother and me without any family. Until I was seventeen and a high school graduate, I was raised in institutions marked by strong emphasis on the importance of order, work, and discipline. The kind of discipline prevailing in these institutions, though sometimes cruel and erratic, was on the whole fair and consistent. The values were stern and puritanical, but they were dependable. The rules were rigorous, but they did not change.

... under tragic circumstances ... I was raised in institutions

It soon became apparent in the analysis that the experience of having my world quite literally shattered at the age of five had made it necessary for me to cling with peculiar intensity to the rules of the institutions in which I lived. I did this as a means of assuring myself of a measure of badly needed security, and as a means, perhaps magical, of warding off some future tragedy that my unconscious told me was fated to overtake me.

Between my experience of life before the age of five, with a father and a mother who were exceptionally warm and affectionate in their natures, and my experience after five in an institutional climate characterized by a lack of warmth and intimacy, there was a gap that could be bridged only with great difficulty. I bridged it, but in ways that contained the seeds of later conflicts. I learned early in life that it was easier to try to secure the approval of others than to try to be myself. I learned that trusting the rules was much safer than trusting my own feelings or the feelings of others.

it was easier to try to secure the approval of others than to try to be myself

One of the rich benefits of a personal analysis is the extensive consideration of dreams. I believe that dreams are, in truth, a gateway to self-understanding. I find now that dreams will tell me much about myself. They have a way of compensating for the excessive face-toward-busyness attitude likely to be so marked a feature of the present-day ministry. We who are ministers do well to recall a line from the Talmud: "A dream which is not understood is like a letter which is not opened." Or we may well remember Emerson's words:

> "Sleep takes off the costume of circumstance, arms us with terrible freedom, so that every will rushes to a deed. A skillful man reads his dreams for his self-knowledge; yet not the details, but the quality."

A dream recurrent during my analysis illustrated one aspect of my particular plight. In this dream, which is concerned with my symbols of office and my role as a preacher, I struggle to put on my academic gown and hood. As I struggle, I know that sermon time is close at hand and that this sermon and this church service from which my recalcitrant gown and hood are holding me back are particularly important. It is especially necessary that I be there, and on time. The urgency of the situation compounds my already high degree of frustration. I finally do get to the church service (a good aspect of my dreaming is that I almost always seem to reach my destination), but I arrive in a state of great exhaustion and anger, worn out by my struggle with the robe and the hood. In one dream of this kind, a woman is dressing me outlandishly and holding me back. She puts a baby bonnet on my head. The bonnet is heavily bordered with lace. When I get to the pulpit and begin my sermon, my voice seems to lisp and whistle as it sounds through the lace. In annoyance and anger, I tear the baby bonnet from my head and proceed with the sermon, feeling much freer and stronger.

It appears that the sermon form I found so frustrating was not only symbolic of the institutional rules that "saved my life" in the early years, though I resented them so much; it may also have been a symbol of the early controls that my mother exercised over me and used for a variety of purposes. Conceivably, in the months leading up to her tragic death, those controls were accentuated. With the loss of my mother and my father, and with their places taken by the orphanage authorities who were the parental surrogates, the controls became impersonal, tighter. Obviously, their tightness and impersonality brought added hazards for a young child's development.

I cannot go into these hazards in detail, but one of them, readily understandable in the light of my situation, was the need to feel grateful, the need to be approved. I had to be grateful as a sign of my appreciation of what they, the authorities, were doing for me. If I was ungrateful, I stood in danger of being cast off, of having my world go to pieces again. Of course, mingled with the "gratitude" was anger, largely unexpressed. And mingled with both these feelings was a deep fear of disapproval. These feelings, appropriate in my relation to the institutions of my childhood, became displaced upon the institutions of adulthood. Sometimes the displacement was appropriate enough, but at other times it was highly inappropriate, and this gave rise to severe problems.

I carried these feelings over in my attitude toward the "demands" of my profession. When in the pulpit, I had the feeling that what I "offered" my congregation—and of course in the analysis this applies also to what I "offered" my analyst—must meet with approval or I was a "bad boy." To be a "bad boy" in my unconscious was hazardous in the extreme. "Bad Boys" get punished, not in any reasonable way, but by having their outward circumstances go to pieces. The sermon thus became a pivotal responsibility, but one that had to be understood in terms of the demands of the past, as well as of the demands of the present. It was the means by which I could secure good grades, desperately needed approval, and security. So, sermon preparation took on the painful character of studying for an examination upon which life itself depended, an examination to be taken, my unconscious told me, under the eye of the harshest kind of taskmaster.

Naturally, it was difficult for me to express with comfort even a normal amount of aggression, because in my unconscious I confused love with submission and healthy aggression with the kind of hatred that courts destruction.

Material in the analysis that related to the death of my mother threw light on elements in the unconscious revealing great anxiety over whether or not I had any right at all to preach. This flowered into my "fear-of-the-empty-cupboard complex." It developed that I felt guilt over the death of my younger brother. The conscious rationale of this guilt was the fact that on the day he drowned, I had expressed to a schoolmate the hope that we would be given the afternoon off from our work. We were given the afternoon off, and the tragedy ensued. I bitterly blamed myself for his death. Back of my harsh self-reproach lay an unusually intense sibling rivalry. It appeared that the guilt experienced here may have screened a deeper source of guilt stemming from my mother's death. It was indicated that unconsciously I felt that much of what had happened to me had happened because of my own badness. Unconsciously, I assumed perhaps that even the loss of my parents was the result of this badness.

I bitterly blamed myself for his death

So it was not surprising that a question basic in the analysis was not how to compose sermons—I did this with satisfactory results. More disturbing for me was the question whether or not I had any right to be composing sermons. Granted that I could perform this task and perform it well, did I have the right to *pretend* to be good?

To put it a bit differently, sermon composition was difficult for me because sermons could lead to self-exposure. To expose a bad self is an unhappy business. Thus, the unconscious aim of sermon preparation had to be self-concealment rather than self-expression. Self-concealment, however, is also bad, because it is a form of dishonesty. So I stood between the devil and the deep blue sea. Sermon composition leads to self-exposure, which is dangerous, or to dishonesty, which is bad. There can, therefore, be no pleasure or deep satisfaction in it.

I spoke earlier of my tendency to regard sermonizing as ecclesiastical feather-bedding and to downgrade the sermon-writing process. There were a good many occasions in the analytic hours when my associations to my sermons were all excremental in character. I constantly downgraded them, regarding them as waste products, taking what comfort I could from the thought that what was excremental might at least have a fertilizing potential. Just about the best thing I could say of one of my homiletic endeavors was that a flower might blossom even from a dunghill!

It was obvious, particularly in the dream material in the analysis, that I displaced much anxiety with regard to sexuality onto sermon preparation. Quite early it became apparent that there was a relation between my difficulty in associating to sexual material and my difficulty with sermon composition. My silences and blockings on these occasions were a product of my lack of acceptance of my feelings and impulses. They stemmed in part from resentment at the analyst for making the same demands on me that were made by my congregation: namely, that I strip myself bare. As a matter of fact, the discipline of free association, which is a primary factor in analysis, was more cruel than preaching. In preaching, one at least had a chance to prepare oneself, which might also be interpreted as a chance to disguise oneself; nor did the rules of preaching deny the right to that choice between alternative thoughts that is our freedom. To practice free association was to say actually what I thought and felt at any given moment, not what someone else wanted me to think or to feel. I found the discipline of free association, exercised through hundreds of hours of analysis, a curious adjunct to hours spent in sermon preparation. I am not yet sure what the carry-over effect will be. As with the steady and consistent practice of meditation, it takes time for the discipline exercised in an analysis to permeate the full personality.

I have mentioned some of the ways in which the personal analysis related to my preaching in order to make the point that psychoanalysis affects professional competency at a deep feeling level. Another minister with a different family constellation and a different life pattern would be affected in different ways.

The positive effect that the analysis had on me in the area of preaching may be summed up as follows: In arriving at a higher degree of self-acceptance and self-knowledge, I resolved, or at least began to see, some of the conflicts underlying the excessive difficulty I experienced in sermon preparation. I became aware, as I have indicated, that many of the uses I was making of sermons or sermonizing were at variance with my conscious intent. I lived through a good many conflicts. I had a good many encounters with my unconscious, which at first I denied were relevant to the problems inherent in sermon composition. But as I lived through these encounters, I began to see that I did have a right to preach, and I began gradually to put a fresher and higher value on the pulpit and its varied meanings. I use the word "began," because the efforts to gain self-knowledge is unending. A psychoanalysis is a beginning and a continuing effort at self-understanding. Freud makes this point in his paper: *Analysis Terminable and Interminable.*[1] There comes a date when one stops seeing one's analyst. There is a merciful termination of the fee-paying privilege. But irrespective of whether or not one returns to the formal analytic process, as Freud suggests, both patient and analyst should from time to time, there is no doubt that the introspective processes and the growth in self-awareness—the increasing appreciation of the unconscious factors present in one's character and personality—are instruments one does not put by with the conclusion of the therapeutic hours. I am aware that my analysis continues to influence me in the tasks of sermon composition. These tasks continue to be difficult, but not *as* difficult. Often, analysis does not remove problems so much as it makes them tolerable and understandable. It provides a vantage point from which to work more intelligently against problems, and this is no small gift or accomplishment.

Psychoanalysis and the understanding of counseling

I now turn to a consideration of the effect that psychoanalysis has had on my own understanding of pastoral counseling. Here I shall be perhaps more speculative, certainly less personal.

I had hoped that an educative analysis would make *completely* clear for me the role of the clergyman in pastoral counseling, and that it would make the problems of pastoral counseling both apparent and transparent. Regrettably, I have not found this to be the case. Analysis has changed my own attitude toward pastoral counseling and also has changed my procedures and techniques somewhat. But I still find it difficult to state what I consider a clergyman's distinctive role as a pastoral counselor to be, and it is only quite recently that I have begun to see certain problems and issues relative to the function of the clergyman as a counselor with any degree of clarity.

I am aware that our need as clergymen to achieve certain practical goals in pastoral counseling often outweighs in our minds the importance of theoretic implications. This puts us in a trap where many disregard theory in favor of practical benefits, as though theory and practice were somehow unrelated. In his brilliant book, *Freud, the Mind of the Moralist,* Philip Rieff raised danger signals for those who are careless of the interrelation between practice and theory. He makes the point that theologians should be extremely careful in subjoining to their theologies such Freudian terms, or the Freudian use of such terms, as "guilt," "anxiety," and "conscience." Freud, he argues, uses these terms in an atheological sense. Reiff is even more concerned lest a blurred and muddy rapprochement between psychoanalysis and religion should take place through, as he puts it, "the affinities which have been discovered between the pastoral techniques of religion and the therapeutic techniques of psychiatry."[2] Rieff is worried—as are other thinkers—lest the identification of pastoral counseling with therapeutic techniques associated with psychoanalysis be an exercise in fuzziness that will ultimately bring discredit and confusion upon both psychoanalysis and the church.

I am impressed by the great need for clarification of roles in this area of practical cooperation. The clergyman is caught between the danger of being too obsequious in his relation to the psychoanalyst, the psychologist, or the psychiatrist, and the danger of endeavoring to emulate the role of the depth psychologist, not because he is capable of such emulation, but because of his fundamental uncertainty and anxiety regarding his own vocation. The two dangers are not unrelated.

I think we need to remember the plurality of viewpoints existing in the psychological camp. As I read the works of psychotherapists such as Erik Erikson, Erich Fromm, Rollo May, Allen Wheelis, and other, I am impressed with the fact that there is a good deal more diversity in the psychoanalytic camp with regard to presuppositions, theories of dynamics, and techniques than we usually assume. I do not mean to imply that there is not a vast body of therapeutic techniques used in common. I do mean to say that there is a large difference between the humanistic psychoanalysis of an Erich Fromm, psychoanalysis as it is set forth by Freud and practiced by the Freudians, and the existentialist therapy delineated and practiced by the Rollo Mays and the Victor Frankls. When you include the clinical psychologies, the spectrum becomes even wider. This pluralism extends through the ranks of psychologists (I use the term "psychologist" as being inclusive of psychoanalysts, psychiatrists, and psychologists).

Carl Rogers, in his book: *On Becoming a Person*, expresses the conviction that "it is the attitudes and feelings of the therapist rather than his theoretical orientation which is important."[3] If we go to the opposite point of view and consider the doctrinaire Freudian with his great stress upon the importance of technique and theoretical orientation, we begin to see how broad the spectrum is. I have not mentioned the difference between the Freudians and the Jungians. My point is that this plurality of approaches to therapy on the part of the psychologists should belie the attitude common among the clergy that the psychologists have one answer to the problem of personality and character disorders that all clergymen should immediately make their own. The pluralistic character of the answers coming out of psychology is something for clergymen to learn from, rather than gloat over.

If there is a good deal of diversity and much questioning going on in the ranks of the psychologists relative to the larger context in which therapy takes place, there is an increasingly sensitive interest in the theological implications of therapy among the theologians. There are also developments in psychotherapy that seem to be bringing the psychologists and the theologians closer together, though not merging them. I am thinking now especially of the existential therapists, with their concentration upon the meaning of existence as being deeply relevant to the health of the person. Ludwig Binswanger describes existentialist psychotherapy in these words:

"A psychotherapy on existential-analytic bases investigates the life-history of the patient to be treated...but it does not explain this life-history and its pathologic idiosyncrasies according to the teachings of any school of psychotherapy, or by means of its preferred categories. Instead it *understands* this life-history as modifications of the total structure of the patient's being-in-the-world."[4]

From a theological perspective, Samuel H. Miller has stated the problem that depth psychology poses for theology in these words:

"Freudian research, as revolutionary as the Copernican theory, has destroyed the equilibrium of modern man. Happening in association with other powerful social and cultural forces, the opening up of vast psychic spaces deep within man's own center has disturbed his relationships at every level of his many-faceted life... We now know that we have not been as much in control of ourselves as we thought, and the powers and mechanisms which have determined our character and overt actions were mysteriously beyond our reach for the most part."[5]

Various contemporary theologians are seeking to come to terms with the problem as Miller outlines it. Let me mention a few who are grappling with it in its theoretic dimensions without ignoring the importance of relating the practical to the theoretic.

The long opening essay by Henry Nelson Wieman in his book, *Intellectual Foundation of Faith*, represents a serious effort to deal with the question: What can save man from his self-destructive propensities?[6] Wieman is concerned to show that religious faith—and his is speaking specifically of liberal religious faith—seeks to meet man both at the level of his creative and destructive propensities and at the level of his unconscious and conscious needs. He contents that liberal religious faith in its true dimensions can meet the challenges posed by the intrapsychic spaces of which Miller writes, and can meet them more strongly and adequately than any other form of religious faith.

Paul Tillich is an even more notable example of a theologian who seeks to bridge the chasm that, for some time, has existed between psychology and theology. He is well aware of the conflict between the two disciplines, but feels that at least part of the responsibility for it lies in the psychologists' camp and in the area of unexamined presuppositions:

> "When faith speaks of the ultimate dimension in which man lives, and in which he can win or lose his soul, or of the ultimate meaning of his existence, it is not interfering at all with the scientific rejection of the concept of the soul. A psychology without soul cannot deny this, nor can a psychology with soul confirm it. The truth of man's eternal meaning lies in a dimension other than the truth of adequate psychological concepts. Contemporary analytic or depth psychology has in many instances conflicted with pretheological and theological expressions of faith. It is, however, not difficult in the statements of depth psychology to distinguish the more or less verified observations and hypotheses from assertions about man's nature and destiny which are clearly expressions of faith. The naturalistic elements which Freud carried from the nineteenth into the twentieth century, his basic puritanism with respect to love, his pessimism about culture, and his reduction of religion to an ideological projection are all expressions of faith and not the result of scientific analyses. There is no reason to deny to a scholar who deals with man and his predicament the right to introduce elements of faith. But if he attacks other forms of faith in the name of scientific psychology, as Freud and many of his followers do, he is confusing dimensions."

This quotation may seem to indicate that Tillich is basically hostile to the findings of depth psychology, but this is not the case. As I read Tillich, he is deeply sensitive to and grateful for the capacity that depth psychology has to correct, clarify, and illuminate theological concepts. I think this recognition of the contribution of depth psychology to theology stands out clearly in his *The Courage to Be*.[8]

Still another theologian of the first rank who talks to the theoretic problems posed in the area of the relation between theology and psychology is Martin Buber. When Buber was in this country a few years ago, he addressed the School of Psychiatry in Washington. Later on, he entered into a discussion with Carl Rogers. He and Rogers found common ground. Rogers recognized, for example, the profundity of Buber's insight into the process by which one person confirms another. Buber writes of this confirming process:

> "Confirming...means accepting the whole personality of the other...I can recognize in him, know in him, the person he has been *created* to become.... I confirm him in myself, and then in him, in relation to this potentiality that...can now be developed, and evolved."[9]

Rogers sees in Buber's insight verification of the insight produced by a group of research psychologists who have been working with schizophrenics in the area of "manufactured relationships." He sees in Buber's insight a verification of hypotheses coming out of his own clinical experiences. My point is that there is a crossing of the lines here. We have one of the most distinguished theologians of the age and one of the most distinguished psychologists learning from one another, exploring the language, their concepts, their experiences in human relationships, to find common ground.

It is apparent that theologians such as Wieman and Buber and Tillich, whom I have named, and others who could be named—Hans Hofmann, Seward Hiltner, Charles A. Curran, and George Hagmaier come to mind—are raising fundamental questions with regard to the interrelations between religion and psychology. These questions pertain to the nature of man, man's relatedness to man, the implications of religious experience and belief for human life. Such theologians raise these questions against a background of sophistication. These men are well-informed about the findings of psychology. In an open spirit, they propose answers to the questions they raise. So there is a dialogue going on between theologians and psychologists.

One of the questions frequently recurring in this dialogue at both the practical and theoretic level is whether or not the clergyman has a unique role. Or, assuming that the role of the minister is different but not unique, what are some of the essential differences between him and the psychologist (using the term "psychologist" in a comprehensive sense)? I offer only very tentatively held points of view here. I am not sure that there is any absolute difference. I am inclined to think that the difference between one psychiatrist and another may be greater than the difference between a particular psychiatrist and a particular clergyman. This applies to schools of theological thought and schools of psychology as well as to individuals. There are basic differences in aim, in technique, in time allotted to treatment, and in training. There are basic differences in categories of thought and interpretation. There are basic differences in what I would call community-representation and community-expectation.

It does not do, I think, to say simply that the clergyman works at the surface of consciousness and the psychologist works in the unconscious depths. Seward Hiltner takes the word "depth" and makes something of a distinction in this area. The psychoanalyst, he points out, may use "depth" to refer to a kind of treatment or treatment process in which he utilizes the method of free association to uncover repressed material stemming from the very earliest experiences of life. He regards these early traumatic experiences as the root causes of character and personality disorder. He directs his attention to pathological conditions and he uses language and concepts that have meaning chiefly in the context of pathology. Hiltner points out that the clergyman may take the same word—depth—and give it a new set of meanings that are as valid for him and his counseling undertakings as the meanings given to the word by the depth psychologists are valid in another sense. By "depth" the clergyman may refer to a parishioner's capacity to set his life in new dimensions. These dimensions would include, on the parishioner's part, a more profound understanding of the nature of good and evil, a fuller acceptance, through an open and daring faith, of the potential goodness of life—what the Psalmist calls "the goodness of God in the land of the living." Seward Hiltner contends that pastoral counseling in depth leads to the asking of the deeper questions of life at both a feeling and an intellectual level; it leads also to a higher dimension of ultimate concerns.[10]

I am aware that there are many ways in which the clergyman is different and set apart from the psychotherapist. I am also aware that, in the therapeutic process as the psychotherapists describe it, there is a mood, texture, uncovering, synthesizing, and a raising of the deep questions that we may describe as "religious." Certainly we would describe them as an experience of ultimate concern, of wonder, and even of worship. Thinkers like Buber and Tillich content that there are moments of "truth" in the psychotherapeutic hours, when the therapist is primarily influential not as a doctor, technician, or professional man, but as a person. There are moments when the deepest meanings of his own life intersect the line of the patient's life. There are moments of I-Thou dialogue. The Swiss psychiatrist, Paul Tournier, in his book, *The Meaning of Persons*, dealing with his own experience as a therapist, makes the same point:

> "There are then two routes to be followed in the knowledge of man: one is objective and scientific, the other is subjective and intuitive. They cannot be equated together, for they require the exercise of utterly different faculties. One proceeds by logical analysis and precise assessment; the other by a total understanding. One is an endless progression; the other is a sudden and complete discovery.

"The two roads do cross, however. Objective exploration prepares the way for the personal encounter, as we have just seen. Conversely, the personal encounter opens the road for more penetrating objective observation. Such is my daily experience, as it is also of those of my colleagues who claim that they are confining themselves strictly to the scientific point of view, though it is a fact that they may not always admit. The personal communion which is established between them and their patients removes psychological "censorship" in the latter, so opening the door to a profounder study of their psychical mechanisms."[11]

I think it would be hard to imagine a more "religious" experience than the one described by Rollo May in excerpts from a patient's case history found in his book, *Existence*. The patient is attempting to say what an experience of being means. It is significant that here is a well-known psychotherapist talking about treatment, psychotherapeutic treatment, in terms of an experience of being; but these are words from the patient herself:

"What is this experience like? It is a primary feeling—it feels like receiving the deed to my house....it is like when as a very young child I once reached the core of a peach and cracked the pit, not knowing what I would find, and then feeling the wonder of finding the inner seed, good to eat in its bitter sweetness....It is like the experience of the poets of the intuitive world, the mystics, except that instead of the pure feeling of and union with God, it is the finding of and the union with my own being. It is like owning Cinderella's shoe and looking all over the world for the foot it will fit and realizing all of a sudden that one's own foot is the only one it will fit. It is like a child in grammar finding the *subject* of the verb in a sentence—in this case the subject being one's own life span. It is ceasing to feel like a theory towards one's self."[12]

Or take another statement, this time from a psychiatrist, not from a patient. It is from Robert C. Murphy's little essay entitled *Psychotherapy Based on Human Longing*."

> "The therapist must know that his work, no matter how 'intuitive,' is nevertheless bound firmly to natural law governing the causal chain of mental processes. For no phenomenon has ever been discovered either of 'matter' or 'spirit,' which escapes from this law, and Freud's rigorous determinism cannot be reversed by all the attacks which offended people have made on it. Man is truly free, in the fullest and most magnificent sense of the word, and it may be conceded that Freud's thought brought him to only the most rudimentary grasp of this truth. But this freedom cannot be discovered on the level of awareness represented by reason, logic, and the scientific discipline to which throughout his life he have such faithful allegiance. Man's freedom is self-evident. It cannot be made 'scientific' or 'proved,' any more than can his existence. It can be apprehended only on the level of understanding which underlies science itself and which makes it possible. Man is free insofar as his life becomes comprehensible to him, and acquires meaning, which is to say: insofar as it expresses his basic longing. It is precisely on this level that the communications between psychotherapist and patient are rooted."[13]

I raise these questions with respect to similarities and dissimilarities as they exist between pastoral counseling and other forms of psychotherapy, as they exist between roles of ministers and psychologists, without having any definitive answers. We are, it seems to me, just beginning to face the problem.

Let me close with a few observations on pastoral counseling.

The essential aim of pastoral counseling is to communicate to another person the sense of the possibility of new

The aim of pastoral counseling is to communicate the sense of the possibility of new being, new life.

being, new life. This new life is born in part out of the dialogue in which the two persons concerned engage, a dialogue that is much more than an exchange of rational, verbalized thought. The clergyman performs a kind of midwife's role, helping the new life to be born, or helping the old life to know its capacity for newness. The midwife analogy breaks down before we carry it very far, because the relation between the clergyman and the parishioner being counseled is such that the clergyman helps to create the new life as well as to bring it forth. Indeed, he and the parishioner create it together.

What the clergyman *is* is more deeply significant than what he knows in an intellectual sense. What he is may be, of course, very different from what the parishioner thinks he is, or even from what he himself thinks he is.

Technique is important. Trying to understand the working of personality and the forces going into the formation of character—trying to understand what has often been called "the interior life"—without knowledge of the techniques utilized by modern psychotherapists, who are in a sense, specialists in the exploration of inner space, is like trying to go into outer space without utilizing the knowledge of the space technologists.

The clergyman speaks out of his own self-awareness

The clergyman speaks out of his own self-awareness.

The clergyman does not force his own coat of armor on to the shoulders of his parishioner. He knows well what would have happened to David if David had been forced to use Saul's armor in the battle against Goliath rather than relying on his own weapons, his own method, his own kind of strength!

The clergyman is open enough to let the parishioner know—and he does not have to do it too obviously—where the mainsprings of his own strength are. This may well involve the sharing of prayer, meditation, readings, vital insights, and personal experiences.

The clergyman will know how to listen.

There is, however, no trick or safe method to make counseling vital. I recall words used by Hans Hofmann in a slightly different connection:

> "The closer we come to the core of what being human means, the less we are prone to need scientific or philosophical approximations. It is painful and frightening to look honestly at life as it really is. The greatest difficulty is to drop our conventional and often hypocritical masks."[14]

There is another side to the story. When one learns to share one's self with another person, sometimes in the midst of the experience there occur happenings infinitely difficult to describe. At times there comes into the counseling process the intention to live. It comes as an integrating element transcending the limits of the two lives that have come together for a time. There can be present in the counseling experience a human longing for wholeness that is poignantly beautiful. Not infrequently, the counselor may feel that his life and the life of the person with him are part of a flowing river rising from the deepest wellsprings of existence. Life is present in frightening and disturbing forms. Life is present also at a depth that evokes love, wonder, and celebration.

*****

NOTES

1. Freud, Sigmund, *Collected Papers*, vol, 5. London, The Hogarth Press, 1950, p. 353.

2. Rieff, Philip, *Freud, the Mind of the Moralist.* New York, the Viking Press, 1959, p. 273.

3. Rogers, Carl R., *On Becoming a Person.* Boston, Houghton Mifflin Co., 1959, p.44.

4. May, Rollo, ed., *Existence*. New York, Basic books, Inc. 1958, p. 5.

5. Hofmann, Hans, ed., *Making the Ministry Relevant*. New York, Charles Scribner's Sons, 1960, pp. 59-60.

6. Wieman, Henry Nelson. *Intellectual foundation of Faith*. New York, Philosophical Library, Inc. 1961, p.1.

7. Tillich, Paul, *Dynamics of Faith*. New York, Harper & Bros., 1957 (World Perspective Series, vol. 10), p. 84.

8. ———, *The Courage to Be*. New Haven, Yale University Press, 1952.

9. Rogers, Carl, *op. cit.*, p. 55.

10. Hiltner, Seward, and Colston, Lowell, G., *The Context of Pastoral Counseling*. Nashville, Tenn., Abington Press, 1961, p. 125.

11. Tournier, Paul, *The Meaning of Persons*. New York, Harper & Bros., 1957, p. 25.

12. May, Rollo, *op.cit.*, p.43.

13. Murphy, Robert C., "Psychotherapy Based on Human Longing," Pendle Hill Pamphlet III, Wallingford, PA, 1960, pp. 8,9.

14. Hofman, Hans, *op. cit.*, p. 16.

MINISTER EMERITUS SINCE 1973
MINISTER FIRST UNITARIAN UNIVERSALIST CHURCH
SAN FRANCISCO 1957-1973
MINISTER FIRST UNITARIAN CHURCH PHILADELPHIA 1947-1957
CHAPLAIN UNITED STATES ARMY 1944-1947

Harry B. Scholefield was born in Massachusetts. Orphaned at an early age, he went on to graduate from Hinckley School, Bowdoin College, Harvard Divinity School, and the Philadelphia Psycho-Analytic Institute. Since becoming a Unitarian minister, he has been awarded honorary degrees from the Meadville Theological School and from the Starr King School for the Ministry as well as a Merrill Fellowship from Harvard Divinity School. He lives north of San Francisco.

Acknowledgement

The publication of these sermons was made possible through the generosity of George Miller to whom I am most grateful. The support of Margot Campbell Gross is also greatly appreciated.

Harry B. Scholefield